Who's in Charge Here?

Humorous Reflections on Our Relationship with God

RUSSELL T. MONTFORT

D0002857

NSIONS
LIVING
VILLE

WHO'S IN CHARGE HERE?
HUMOROUS REFLECTIONS ON OUR RELATIONSHIP WITH GOD

Copyright © 2006 by Dimensions for Living

All rights reserved.
No part of this work may be reproduced or transmitted in any form or by any
means, electronic or mechanical, including photocopying and recording, or by any
information storage or retrieval system, except as may be expressly permitted by
the 1976 Copyright Act or in writing from the publisher. Requests for permission
can be addressed to Dimensions for Living, P.O. Box 801, 201 Eighth Avenue
South, Nashville, TN 37202-0801, or emailed to permissions@umpublishing.org.

This book is printed on acid-free paper.

Library of Congress Cataloging-in-Publication Data

Montfort, Russell T., 1928-
  Who's in charge here? : humorous reflections on our relationship with God /
Russell T. Montfort.
    p. cm.
  ISBN 0-687-49685-3 (binding: adhesive, perfect : alk. paper)
  1. Christian life—Humor. I. Title.
  BV4517.M65 2006
  248.402'07—dc22

10-25.08

2006012592

All scripture quotations are taken from the *New Revised Standard Version of the
Bible,* copyright 1989, by the Division of Christian Education of the National
Council of the Churches of Christ in the United States of America. Used by per-
mission. All rights reserved.

06 07 08 09 10 11 12 13 14 15—10 9 8 7 6 5 4 3 2 1

MANUFACTURED IN THE UNITED STATES OF AMERICA

Contents

Introduction

ERE IS A COLLECTION OF SOME OCCASIONAL PIECES THAT are, in a way, part of a now-and-then journal of my adult years after I began to discover the ambiguity with which we all process what's happening in our lives. I started remembering and writing down some of the stories in which truth was told or acted out in unexpected ways.

The people of my first parish were for the most part farmers or mill workers. Some worked in knitting or furniture factories. They were kind and loving people who lived in tight little communities. They were mostly kin to one another and spoke in a distinct vernacular. Early on, I realized that in the stories they told, and in the metaphors they used, there were clues to their interior lives and information that would help me understand them as well as get insight into my own life.

Mrs. Kennedy was the mother of six grown children whose family liked to go to the beach, which was the chosen vacation destination for most people like themselves. As a matter of fact, some plants and factories closed for the week of July Fourth and many of the workers converged at the same time on the beaches of North and South Carolina. One year, running up to the Fourth, Mrs. Kennedy confided in me that she didn't like to go to the beach; looking at that water reminded her of all "those boys who crossed that ocean" during World War II "who never came back. They died over there." At first it seemed to be a pitiable saying out of the mouth of an eccentric old woman but upon reflection, I understood. To her that sea was no thing of beauty; it was no place to vacation. It was a menacing force that went someplace she had never seen and couldn't quite imagine. And out there somewhere, it threw itself up on another shore where young men went to die. They died there by the thousands on the beaches of Normandy. That was the same ocean that surged up on the North Carolina beach where her family went to play. It was a mean and onerous thing.

I saw that I could be no friend to her unless I tried to hear her stories, help her get them told, help her understand why she felt so miserable and alone in her big family, especially while vacationing at the beach.

Within a day or two of my exchange with Mrs. Kennedy, another of my flock called. A lady wanted me to stop by her house; she had a "vision" to discuss with me. She had been ill for years, spending much of her life in bed, and she told me that Jesus and Paul had come and stood at the foot of her bed the night before. Jesus she described as a tall man, and Paul was a "little low feller." It was Paul, she said, who did most of the talking. She told me about some details of the conversation which I no longer recall but to which I responded, "Was it a good visit? Were you happy they were here?" She replied, "Oh my, yes, I hope they will come again."

I really cherished the detail of her description of Paul as a know-it-all, doing all the talking as he does in the New Testament. What did her dream or vision mean? I don't know but she had experienced the Holy and it made her feel good, which was something she hadn't felt in a long time and something to which I felt I should pay attention.

Most twenty-first-century people are prosy people, which is too bad because the language of religion is the language of symbol, myth, and metaphor—the language of poetry. In all of the Gospels except that of John, when Jesus had something important to say, he often told a story and he would begin, "The kingdom of God is like a householder who . . ." He compared God's concerns for individual persons to a woman who lost a coin. He spoke of God's interest in lost persons as that of a shepherd who had lost a sheep. Jesus certainly did not mean that God is a female shepherd who owns a house.

In the following stories, I am not presenting parables but my intent is to break open some usual ways of saying things. We will sometimes look for a new vocabulary. Occasionally, as did Jesus, I will tell a story and leave it to you to give it meaning.

I have an adage with which I sometimes assess events and situations. I say to myself, "What's happening is not necessarily what's going on." I fear that prosy people see what's happening, but they often are unable to tell you what's going on.

These comments and stories follow no special order but they are sometimes hooked to the year's seasons. Mostly, they grow out of everyday happenings. Pretty much the way life happens. They are about Christmas and baptisms and world affairs and school and children at play. They are about work and politics and some ordinary people who live life with flair. And a few are about some who never get it; that is, who never really understand what's going on.

1. Who's in Charge Here?

D O YOU EVER GET THE IMPRESSION THAT NO ONE IS IN charge? When I was a child, I knew that there were adults in charge of the school, the school bus, the playground, and certainly in my house, where they said things like, "Sit up straight!" "Get your elbows off the table!" and "Don't run in the house!"

When I was a university student, there were people in charge who said intimidating things like "Tomorrow is your last drop/add day!" "You may not enter the dining room at dinner unless you are wearing a tie and jacket!" and "If you cut class the day before or after a holiday, that amounts to a double cut!"

And then I became a pastor, and there were people in charge who said things like "No church should ever report at the end of the year that no one was received on profession of faith!" and "Your [pastoral] appointment is the Thomasville Circuit [four churches with a total of 1,200 members in three counties]"!

I used to think that there were people in charge of every-thing and though sometimes they didn't do things the way I would do them, there was some comfort in knowing that someone was thinking about things.

That was before I grew up. I realize now that no one has the foggiest notion about how the stock market works and why it goes up and down. They say they do, but they don't. And land developers don't know what they are doing. They run out and buy land and build things on it and maybe some-body will buy it and maybe they won't. Even presidents of the United States shade things so that they could mean more than one thing. One president, having been accused of some scandalous behavior with a couple of young women, in response to a question involving the word *is* said, "That all depends on what your definition of *is* is." And another said that we should go to war against Iraq because Iraq had weapons of mass destruction when they didn't. So he went to war anyway, and said it was to further democracy in the world.

Marxist socialism, we were told, was our most feared enemy and then one day it just died right there in front of us, and while most people knew it was sick, almost nobody knew it was terminally ill.

Anyway, now I know. We live in a "maybe" world. And I don't feel all that bad about it because now I understand with clarity that we are, all of us, improvising much of the time. It is the human condition and it is actually exciting to discover that I am not totally controlled by and victimized by the decisions of others. I have been called into a cocreating role with God. God wants me to help get things done. God needs me to think about things and get things done.

It doesn't mean, of course, that I must do it all myself. I will find a community of persons with whom to share the tasks and develop strategies. That adds to the fun. But now that I know there is not somebody out there who is going to fix everything, I realize all the more how important I am. And how important you are.

We are in charge.

2. Telling Stories

ONE OUGHT TO MOVE NOW AND THEN JUST TO BE FORCED to clean out the closets and dresser drawers. And the desks. I'm a card saver—you know: birthday cards, anniversary cards, get-well cards, and Christmas cards. There is something very personal about the most impersonal card. I see more than the signature. I wonder why that person chose that card. And it is generally true that the sender's choice of card somehow is expressive of the sender.

We are moving. From one house to another. From a larger house to a smaller house and that means the cards have to go, but it is very hard to get through the cards without experiencing some significant feelings. They are more than cards to be disposed of. They evoke special occasions or simply give little reminders of one's own half-forgotten past, not to mention some major laughs.

I reread one from several years back that is delicious. These friends had moved to Barcelona, Spain, from the

U.S.—sent there by the husband's company—and the wife was reinventing her life when she sent their Christmas card.

On the front was a photograph of the entire family, snapped in some obviously exotic spot. And with it came a handwritten letter describing just how hectic and absolutely extraordinary was the life they lived, though taking Spanish lessons every day and maintaining the rigorous social and business life of the family of an employee of a multinational corporation was punishing.

The best line was: "The picture on the card was taken on the island of Crete during a little Mediterranean cruise thing we did during the children's school holiday."

Somebody ought to do a book of these things. I have a lot of others, the best of which was delivered by a genealogist in a letter to my sister-in-law when she wrote to him to inquire about some relatives that we and he shared. He answered promptly and said somewhere in the body of his letter he had been thinking about that very ancestor a few days earlier "as I was diving off the back of my boat while anchored in Long Island Sound." He's good. That's in the league with "little Mediterranean cruise thing."

My wife and children are merciless and won't let me do that. I love to do it, but they intimidated me with wild whoops of laughter once when I casually dropped into the conversation something about "the last time I was in Lucerne."

Maybe we all do it. Reinvent ourselves as we tell our stories, redefine our philosophy of life as we remember the things that happened to us. Some theologians now insist that we are doing theology as we remember and tell our stories. How they happened and what they mean. And that God probably doesn't become real to us until we somehow are able to read our own story and discover both patterns and special revelations there.

I think there is much to be said for such a theory. If we cannot detect God at work in our own lives, God doesn't mean much. God remains an inaccessible abstraction. Part of God's story (according to the Bible) is that God wanted a relationship with us and so God came among us as one of us so that we didn't have to deal with abstraction only, and now lives among us as indwelling Spirit. I like that version of God's story.

Now, sorting out what is happening from what is merely going on remains a significant task. What would probably help us most is to be able to recall all of the Christmas letters and now-and-then correspondence that we sent to others with the sole purpose of reshaping our lives according to some preconceived notion of what we thought others would find most impressive. Recover them and see what we thought of our own lives.

We have to be careful, of course, with our autobiographical narratives or we might end up like Michael Jackson—an entirely made-up person who seems to think he is Peter Pan, when in actuality he is Tinkerbell.

Enough of that. Back to the cards and back to moving. It is difficult to trash your past. It is all tied up in the stuff you accumulate.

3. A Boy's Best Friend

WHEN I WAS GROWING UP IN RURAL KENTUCKY, WE HAD two dogs, Bucky and Louie. Bucky we named for Bucky Walters, who was a star player for the Cincinnati Reds baseball team. Bucky the dog was a hustler like Bucky the baseball player. And Bucky the dog was full of energy, funny, and up for anything you wanted to do—fetch a stick, go swimming in the creek, gather up the cows, or just goof around.

Louie was as pitiful-looking a dog as you ever saw. He was dirty white all over with the exception of one ear, which was yellow. He had permanent grass stains. And instead of big laughing eyes like Bucky's, he had little beady eyes that made him look sinister, as if he were planning to kill a sheep or something.

And Louie was not into a lot of dog stuff. He would fetch the stick the first time you threw it, but when you threw it again, he would sit down and look at you like, "Say what?" And he never barked at strangers and he slept at night in the porch swing. He even knew how to make it swing. All night long you could hear this swing going back and forth. And he never came when we called him to eat. He would act as if he had no interest at all in what you put out for him but woe unto Bucky if he tried to eat out of Louie's dish. Louie was not charmed by Bucky's enthusiastic, happy-family-pet act.

When no one was looking, Louie ate his supper. He just wanted everyone to know that he wasn't one of those dogs that bounded all around you and wanted to lick your face and show you how wonderful you are. Louie had his own persona and better for you when you learned his drill.

He was imperious, proud, and insolent with absolutely nothing to be imperious, proud, and insolent about. He despised Bucky, all the cats, and especially this big Plymouth Rock rooster who was headman in the chicken yard. When the people weren't looking, he liked running that rooster ragged. Everybody in our family was afraid of Louie.

Except Paul. Paul was my brother, ten years younger than I, and the littlest member of our household. And the way Louie ruled the yard, Paul ruled the house (without the terror factor, of course). He was about three years old when I remember him best with Louie. He would fix a rope around Louie's neck and take him for a walk. Louie would go. Paul would put Louie in a tub and give him a bath and we watched in wonder, because Louie would stand there and take it. He would narrow those beady little eyes down even further, but there was no protest. And once I came through the gate, and there sat Paul, on top of Louie, recumbent. Paul was building something out of sticks, and Louie was his sitting place. No growls, no bared teeth, just a sweet resignation. It was remarkable.

You see, Louie loved Paul and that was the difference. Love always acts like that. Long-suffering and patient. And forgiving. Paul and Louie resonated, as some say.

Love is powerful. It was the only thing that could pierce Louie's impenetrable self and turn him into a boy's best friend.

4. A Big Little Book

FREDERICK BUECHNER WAS READING AN EXCERPT FROM HIS book *A Wizard's Tale* at a writers' workshop that I attended one weekend, and he just casually alluded to Big Little Books. He is a man whose age approximates mine, and *A Wizard's Tale* is a fictionalized account of his childhood.

I remember Big Little Books. Very aptly named. As thick as a Michener book but all chopped off and trimmed down until it was nearly thicker than it was wide and tall. And as Buechner read on, my memory bank coughed up an event in my own childhood in which a Big Little Book was prominently featured.

My family and I were on our way to visit my grandmother, who lived about a hundred miles from our house. For some unremembered reason, I decided to mark the way to Grandmother's house by tearing the pages out of my Big Little Book and dropping them, one at a time, out the window. I rationed them very carefully over the two-and-one-half hours it took to make the journey. I didn't so much reason as fantasize that we would see welcoming little white flashes of paper in the headlights in our after-dark return that would indicate we were on the right road back.

Just as we returned to the car for the trip home, my mother saw the empty hard covers of my Big Little Book thrown on the floor of the backseat of our 1934 Ford. She inquired as to how it got that way and I reported to her how I thought we would have the comfort of seeing that long white flashing trail back to our house. There was little romance in my mother's psyche. In her glossary of ways to get to and fro, she knew only roadmaps and posted signs. She didn't realize that by dropping a trail of crumbs or flower petals, or that by marking trees or leaving little piles of stones, you could also get home.

Anyway, I was punished. I don't remember the exact form of the punishment, but usually it came swift and sure, and had something to do with razor strops and switches. And I admit that I never again tore up a book.

Fortunately, Mama was never able to rid me of my hopeless infatuation with the mystery and romance of life. Some glimmers remain. And so I can still be overwhelmed by moments of beauty and truth and song when they break through the everydayness of roadmaps and place signs.

It really is not a good thing to tear up a book. Books are treasures. Not all books, but many. But then it's probably not a good idea to step on a child's imagination either and humiliate him into prosaic perceptions of and pedestrian responses to life.

After all this time, I keep thinking of Big Little Books. If I had a few, I could probably make a hundred dollars off of them at the flea market or be featured on *Antiques Roadshow*. Mama would like that.

5. Spoon Bread

WE SAT DOWN TO DINNER IN THEIR ELEGANTLY APPOINTED dining room. Good English antiques, linen, silver, and candlelight. And a male cook, who had first prepared the meal and was now serving it. I was no more than twenty years old, and in Ballardsville, Kentucky, you didn't see a lot of English antiques and linen, much less a bona fide cook who also waited table.

I was hoping to do the right thing when the cook offered me the spoon bread. The hostess made some appropriate remark about the spoon bread being the cook's best dish. He was known for it. All over.

Well, not exactly all over—I didn't know it. I didn't even know what spoon bread was, much less how you got it out of the pan. He offered it to me first. I'm sure he saw the terror in my eyes because he looked as if he really wanted to help. He was smiling but it was not a disdainful or patronizing smile. It was more like, "Think quickly. You can do it!" But I couldn't and so I refused.

Then I watched the others spoon it out on their plates and ladle melted butter from a little silver boat onto it. As the cook circled the table and I heard the other guests' exclamations of appreciation, I wanted some of that stuff. But having refused it once, I thought I couldn't go back. Thereby keeping my cool image intact, but paying the price of the hot-buttered spoon bread.

Most of us do that. A lot. Creating images of ourselves and then living them out. Sometimes expanding those images into an entire history that may never have been so, or at best was only partly so. And the irony of it all is that you can really fool other people, and even yourself. But probably not for always. Down inside, there is this nagging fear that the real you may get out and embarrass you.

Once, when I was a child, we had overnight guests. At breakfast the next morning, as my mother removed the platter that had held the fried eggs, my brother yelled out, "Mama, give me a biscuit, I'm gonna sop that egg plate!" I was mortified! But then you might expect that from a child who was in training to become a man who would pass up the best-known dish in the entire area, just because he was afraid to say, "That looks wonderful, but I don't know how to get it out of the pan."

There is an acceptable place to stand, somewhere between the gaucherie of a preadolescent at a farm breakfast table and the frightful anxiety of an uptight pseudosophisticate at a candlelit dinner.

And it has something to do with being willing, on occasion, to look a little foolish or be wrong or simply not know. And to know that not knowing is OK. It makes life easier for you and, believe it or not, it actually endears you to others. Who are struggling with their own uncertainties. Not to mention the fact that you totally miss out on the spoon bread.

6. Cordie

I T WAS SUNDAY, AND THE DAY WAS BLISTERING HOT. I HAD
been in that parish for about eight months and was
beginning to feel more comfortable. But they had never
had a pastor as young as I, single and seminary educated,
and they weren't sure who I was. I talked differently,
dressed differently, and drove a sporty car with lots of
chrome on it.

I was greeting worshipers at the conclusion of Sunday
morning worship. I never was quite sure why preachers did
that but it seemed to be a universal behavior so I did it too.
Most people regularly got in the line, not because they understood any better than I, but because it was expected. Nothing
much of importance was ever said but it was an actual eye-
to-eye encounter that we might not otherwise have had.

I had been at it a while when I extracted a handkerchief
from my coat and wiped the perspiration from my hands.
There was no air-conditioning and I had already perspired

through the back of my jacket and the waist-band of my trousers, and my shirt was wet. The knot of my tie had darkened with sweat.

In one motion, I wiped my hands and put the handkerchief in my pocket. In that gesture, I turned enough to see Cordie standing about ten feet away watching me.

She was a farm wife who had a lot of children, a number of sons and one daughter. She was short and round and wore a frazzled little hat that looked as if it had a storied life of its own. Cordie always wore a broad smile and sometimes dyed her hair a vivid orange color. In the brief moment when our eyes met, I acknowledged her happy face, we nodded, and I went back to the task at hand.

As the worshipers finished their good-byes and walked to their cars, I looked up and away, and again caught the eye of Cordie. She was still standing in the same position wearing the same beneficent smile.

She spoke. "I think you are the purtiest thing I ever saw."

It was a benediction. I did not for a moment think I was the prettiest thing she had ever seen. What I heard her say was that she liked me. I was different and the topic of much community conversation and she had watched me at work, watched me sweat, even understood in some enigmatic way my unease and called out to me that I was the prettiest thing she had ever seen. I thanked her and we stood there momentarily, smiling, and then went on with our lives, enriched by the mutual admiration we shared.

7. Never Always

LOVE FOLK SPEECH. IT'S OFTEN WISE AND OFTEN POETIC. Little homemade signs in store windows are sometimes the best examples of all. Joe Creason was a columnist for the *Louisville Courier-Journal* who wrote one day about such a sign in the window of a central Kentucky family-owned restaurant. In his story, all eventualities seemed covered in that sign: "We open promptly every day at 6, usually."

That statement is actually more the way life is lived than if the message went out without its qualifying last word. Folks tend to speak with such dogmatism at times when, as a matter of fact, there are a lot of absolutes that need to be conditioned.

My wife, Ruth, and I discovered a long time ago that our personal conversations in which we disagree tend to turn out better if we forego the use of such words as *always* and *never*. In all likelihood, the most effective use of those words might be, "Never say never and always avoid always."

I think it was during some marriage enrichment exercises devised by David and Vera Mace that we learned those are heavily freighted words that are characteristic of Style II conversation, which is to be avoided at all costs in interpersonal transactions.

Style II, according to the Maces, is "the style in which you assert yourself and try to dominate or manipulate the other person. . . . It is used to blame, to demand, to control, to put down. You use it when you are trying to force the other person to change or to surrender" (*How to Have a Happy Marriage* [Nashville: Abingdon Press, 1977], 83-84).

Style II has "a sting in its tail" and tends to put others on the defensive and elicits a Style II response. About the only thing left to do is fight.

I think that the proprietors of a restaurant that opens "promptly every day at 6, usually" are people who can be trusted and they probably serve good food, most of the time.

8. Seeming

PEOPLE TEND TO TREAT PREACHERS FUNNY. NOT FUNNY ha-ha, but funny peculiar. I have spent most of my professional life trying not to surprise people with the real me. Not because I'm ashamed of the real me but because I think most people don't want to see the real me. Who isn't all that bad. As one man in my congregation said to his friend, "You really ought to get to know Montfort. He's nicer than he seems."

I'm not sure I know what that means but I think it has something to do with the way people act around church. They act funny. Preachers do it better than anyone, got up in their robes and with their pear-shaped tones. Most of them are nicer and more accessible than they seem.

What to do? I find lots of people around church strongly motivated by service but afraid they will have to assume certain airs and abide by certain rules in order to get on with it. And they don't know the jargon. So they just don't get involved.

Except sometimes they do. In one town where I once served, the mayor of the town was a regular attendee at worship, joining his wife and children there. One year, raising money was a problem, and the congregation had not paid the preacher what they had promised. A congregational meeting was called and several members spoke, using churchified words such as *stewardship, commitment, apportionments,* and *missional priorities.*

About then is when the mayor got up. He spoke with a slight stutter and what he said was, "Now l-l-look here. We said we were going to p-p-pay the preacher this much, now b-b-by damn, we're going to pay him." Then he announced that he was going to take up an offering, which he did, and there was enough to pay the preacher and some left over. Meeting adjourned.

It would be much nicer if we all admitted who we are down deep inside, and, accepting that in one another, got on with it. I have had the pleasant discovery that a lot of lay-people are nicer than they seem under their prearranged faces and nice manners.

In her book *Gilead,* Marylynne Robinson has the old preacher say, in a letter to his son:

> That's the strangest thing . . . about being in the ministry. People change the subject when they see you coming. And

then those very same people come into your study and tell you the most remarkable things. There's a lot under the surface of life, everyone knows that. A lot of malice and dread and guilt, and so much loneliness, where you wouldn't really expect to find it, either. (Marilynne Robinson, *Gilead* [New York: Farrar, Strauss and Giroux, 2005], 6)

9. That Night

DID I EVER TELL YOU ABOUT THE TIME I FELL INTO THE Christmas tree? It isn't done easily. You have to be about six years old and while you are jumping on the sofa, you lose your balance and fall over the arm of the sofa and into the Christmas tree. Head first. Which does not endear you to your mother nor your Aunt Irene, whose Christmas tree and sofa it is.

I had to go to the doctor to get a piece of cedar out of my eye. Fortunately, the doctor lived downstairs and, while I had this scratchy feeling in my eye for several days thereafter, I was able to go on with the holiday. The Christmas tree, however, looked wanly unfestive with some of its branches broken and a number of its ornaments shattered, which condition was explained to everyone who came in by saying that was "where Russell fell in the Christmas tree."

In retrospect, I realize that Christmas was for the most part a misunderstood experience for me. I can't say that I didn't like it. I just didn't understand it. I knew what it was about.

It was about Jesus and his birth but that wasn't in my head. What was in my head was gifts and getting out of school.

We didn't go to church on Christmas. I think that not many Protestant people did in our part of rural Kentucky. We were Protestant people. Now and then. And what Protestant people did in their churches at Christmastime was to have a program in which children sang songs or did recitations (which we called "pieces," as in "I have a piece to say"). When it was all over, adults handed out bags of candy, nuts, and fruit to all the children. But the candy was hard candy and I didn't like that.

One year at our church, my cousin O.J. was to give the opening piece. It was announced as "Welcome by O.J. Smith," and he strode purposefully to the front of the sanctuary (known in those precincts as the auditorium), mounted the steps, turned to face the audience, and said, "I don't know mine!" Then he went back to his seat.

I was stunned at what O.J. did. I didn't know you could do that. Nobody said a word. I don't remember ever hearing anybody in the family discuss it. Nobody seemed to think less of him for it. It was assigned to that body of things never discussed in our family, like sex and in-laws.

Other than falling in the Christmas tree and O.J.'s "piece" that wasn't, I don't have any really stellar memories of Christmases past as a child. I do remember when we got lights for our tree. There were three strings of lights, seven bulbs each. That was twenty-one lights. It nearly drove me crazy if two bulbs of the same color were side by side. While my mother was out of the room, I would rearrange the bulbs in a more pleasing pattern. The tree stood in front of a window so I would go outside in the dark to see how it looked from out there. And if it didn't meet my standards, I would go inside and move the bulbs some more. My Aunt Elizabeth caught me at it once and, laughing, she commented on how easily offended was my "aesthetic sense." That was the first time I had heard that word. I quickly co-opted it into my vocabulary and, though mildly embarrassed at being caught at such a foolish business, I was secretly pleased to be perceived as having an "aesthetic sense."

I do have a Christmas memory that started out darkly. I was sixteen; it was during World War II and my older brother Scott was in Europe in the army. My father, who was old enough to be our grandfather, was terribly troubled over Scott's safety. As a consequence of his anxiety, he drank to excess and mostly slept. My little brother had early on escaped into a world of make-believe—a universe of his own construct, populated by imaginary friends with whom he played. He mostly stayed in his room but you could hear him talking to his "friends." My mother was essentially sad, and on this particular Christmas Eve she worked alone in the kitchen. And I was so busy inventing myself that I lived a life that mostly went unreported.

I had heard that there was a midnight service in a

Presbyterian church in a nearby town. I didn't get off my job at Barr's Grocery in LaGrange until after 10:00 P.M., but I determined that I would do that. Go to that church. That night. I went home, passed through, changed my clothes, and drove to the next town.

I don't remember anything that was said. What was said was only incidental to what was happening. I had never seen a choir in robes—white surplices over black cassocks—and the church was candlelit and there were poinsettias stuck here and there. Even though it was a small church, in the half-dark you couldn't see much. There was an aura like that seen when you look through the windshield of your car on a rainy night. Shapes were distorted and there was movement among the people and the candle flames danced in response to any movement of air and there was smoke from the candles and an amalgam of voices singing and the organ playing.

And for the first time I experienced the mystery. The mystery of the event—of the Holy God coming among us. Rationality stepped aside and I was affected mysteriously. It was a holy night; it was one of those experiences that becomes a touchstone thereafter, one to which you return again and again and by which you evaluate later epiphanies.

It still happens to me. On Christmas Eve, when I look into the expectant faces and hear the songs, I am caught up in an ecstasy. Expectancy. Maybe tonight. Maybe this night, he will come. Christ will come. I am changed.

10. The Cat

MELVIN WAS A BAD-TEMPERED, ARROGANT CAT OWNED by our small son. One might venture that he was psychotic; I once saw him attack an automobile, jumping on it and clawing it furiously. At the time, three very serious dons of academe and I were sitting in it.

At other times he would sit on the mantel, sphinx-like, unblinking and rigid like a piece of porcelain waiting for some unheeding and pounceable human to pass.

And there were the nights when he and his friends gathered outside my bedroom window to howl and whine and fight until daybreak. That's what did him in. Or perhaps better said, that's what did me in. At first light one morning, I said to Ruth, "That's it! Not one more night!"

As soon as the children were off to nursery school, I threw that varmint into the back of the car and headed for some remote outlying area. I backed out of the driveway and turned south, waving to Ruth, who was standing on the porch waving back and laughing. Melvin was sitting beside her, washing down his ruffled fur. The back window of the car was open.

Back in the driveway. Roll the window up. Retrieve Melvin. Leave again. Drive to the country. Put Melvin out. Leave that malevolent, disobliging feline to whatever elements there were.

By the time I arrived back in our little town, remorse had set in. I couldn't believe I had done that—that I had allowed myself to succumb to frustration over the fact that I could not control this ornery cat. Maybe, I thought, my frustration had something to do with my inability to control my own orneriness. In that philosophical funk, I went into the house and confessed my guilt to Ruth.

"Ms. Martin," she said (in her condescending elementary teacher voice), "would like to have Melvin. She would like to take him to her family's farm." Ms. Martin kept house for the people next door.

To give you some perspective, I need to tell you that the elderly people who lived in the house next door and employed Ms. Martin to cook and clean for them were also very frugal. Ms. Martin made fresh biscuits every morning for breakfast. But there were always biscuits left over from the morning previous. They were to be eaten first. So the people always ate day-old biscuits. And by the way, the old man had a cow that he liked to graze in his front yard. He would sit in a rocking chair on his porch and hold a rope tethered to the cow while she cut his grass and did other "cowy" things. And that should give you insight into the collateral craziness in which we lived. We did not need a manic cat.

I went back to the car, drove the eight or nine miles to the scene of the crime, and tried calling Melvin back. Foolish exercise. He hated me as much as I hated him, and he may have been mean but he wasn't stupid. He wasn't up for any more rides with the Godfather.

Back to town. Draw a map. Send Ruth. She was back in an hour with Melvin. He and I avoided one another's gaze. Five hours had passed and we were right back where we began. But by night he was gone. To the farm.

While hanging on the car, out there in the wilds, calling, "Here kitty, kitty, kitty," I had some insights. It's a lot harder to undo or call back a misdeed than to perpetrate it in the first place. Especially when one's pride is involved. When an occasional car would pass, I would look up toward the trees and pretend I was assaying that stand of timber. And because there was a farmhouse not too distant, I couldn't call too loudly. And besides that, I didn't really care what happened to Melvin. It was I who concerned me most—the kind of guy who abuses animals.

Anger, frustration, and pride had done me in. And I had no ability to undo the dirty deed. I had to find an intercessor and wait for grace. Always humbling and always healing.

The last time I heard from Melvin, someone had taken a fancy to him and he was living rather well in Baltimore.

11. Larry

L ARRY WAS ONE OF A PAIR; THEY WERE TWINS. THEY
arrived on campus the same year that I did. They were
students and I was pastor of a church at the campus.
They were privileged and urbane. They had been brought up
in a mainline Protestant church, but by the time I got them
they had assumed outside sniper positions and spent a lot of
time brilliantly miming church people in general and specif-
ically their parents. Their banter was mocking and derisive;
it was also shamelessly but hilariously on-target.

Nevertheless they became regulars in our student group
that met every Friday night for dinner, and Larry in particular began to take his faith seriously. He joined our
congregation.

It was in the late 1950s and early 1960s, and the Civil
Rights movement was beginning to assert itself in the public arena. It was no longer possible to think about human
rights in the abstract. It was an issue that was characterized
by its immediacy. It would not be postponed, and people of

faith had differing opinions as to how it should be addressed. There was no allowance for neutrality.

Larry became assertive in his insistence that people of all races should be treated with equity. He had never had any social interaction with African Americans, as most of us had not. He wanted our group to invite blacks to our meetings, to our worship. He wanted discourse.

We did, and every encounter was dynamite. It was instructive for me to watch the students find their way with young black men and women who were exactly their age. The conversations wove through verbal minefields just waiting for a misstep. The word *nigra* set off the first volley; it was what upper-class whites said when they meant to be polite. For those students, that single encounter most likely dropped the word *nigra* from their lexicon of socially acceptable ways of talking to and about Negro people. The terms *black, African American,* and *people of color* had not yet worked their way into popular usage. They came later.

One black student raised in Mississippi told a story of her mother, a teacher with a master's degree, having to wait until every other customer in a dime store had been served before she could step up to the counter. The clerk was a white teenager; she addressed the teacher by her first name, "Mary." The student wept as she spun out the tale of her mother's humiliation.

Incidents of confrontation and interracial hostility began to pop up nationwide but with special rancor and contrariness in our part of the country. Fear and uncertainty often ruled public discourse as many of us tried to do what was right—to discern what was right, what was possible.

Larry was bright and thoughtful, and he got his convictions ordered and sorted quicker than most of us. It was inspiring for me to watch him and others move from abstraction to action in their response to racism.

Summer came, and the students went home to jobs or travel or summer studies in other places. It was a good time for me to switch to a less demanding schedule, and it was time for the meeting of my denomination's annual conference, the regional group of churches to which we belonged.

A petition was presented to the conference by a group of pastors. The conference center had a swimming pool, and those whose duty it was to make policies regarding the governance of that place had made a statement that the swimming pool would not be integrated; black people could not swim there. The petition asked that the rule be overturned.

When the issue came to the floor for a vote, there were opinions stated on both sides, and when the question was called, the petition was approved.

Then the presiding bishop stepped to the podium and announced that he wanted to step outside his position as bishop and speak to the issue. Granted that privilege, he declared that he was against any denial of educational opportunity for Negro people and that he was for economic equity for all people regardless of race. "But," he said, "when it comes to little white boys and girls and little black boys and girls putting on their bathing suits and playing around in the water in my backyard, that's where I draw the line!"

He returned to his seat as the presiding officer and the other business of the conference went on, but there was no energy in the room. It was as if all the oxygen had been sucked out of the place. It was hot and there was no breeze. There was a somber quiet—almost disbelief at what had happened.

Summer ended; it was mid-September. The students began to drift back in. I was in my office at the church, the door standing open; I heard a knock. I turned to see Larry, unsmiling. He had just returned to campus after a summer in Provence. I stood and greeted him and invited him in. We sat and almost immediately he unfurled a newspaper article dated from early in June. Someone had saved it for him.

It was an account of the action at the church conference when the vote was taken urging those in charge of the conference center to desegregate their swimming pool. It also reported the bishop's personal statement, word for word.

Larry asked, "Did he say that? Did the bishop really say that?" And I answered that he did; he really said that.

He looked at me for a moment without speaking and then stood and said, "Russ, I love your Jesus, but damn your church! Take my name off the roll." And he left.

12. Remembering

I SERVED A CHURCH IN WINSTON-SALEM, NORTH CAROLINA, called Burkhead United Methodist Church. It was named for a former pastor, L. S. Burkhead, whose portrait hung just inside the main entrance to the church. You couldn't get in or out of that church without passing that picture. And he was an intimidating presence. He had been, obviously, a man of faith and insight and persuasive powers. But ugly. He had a heavy square jaw fringed with a long straight gray beard that seemed to be growing out of his neck. There was not a trace of a smile but steely eyes that pierced you. You always felt that you needed to stop and explain something to him. About where you had been and what you had been doing. And why you hadn't come sooner.

Anyway, we built a new church in another part of the city, and in the confusion of that move, we never got around to hanging the Reverend Burkhead again. We found places for all the other former pastors, but after carrying that thing around and trying it in all sorts of places, it seemed always to end up in the closet. With all the mops and the floor wax and the folding tables.

One Sunday afternoon, I had to go back to the church in the early afternoon. My eight-year-old son walked with me, and we encountered on the front steps a very elegant gentleman and his patrician lady companion. He removed his grey fedora hat and introduced himself and the lady. They were both justices of the North Carolina Supreme Court—at the time, he was the chief justice. Later, she became the chief justice.

He identified himself as a nephew of the late L. S. Burkhead and he knew that a portrait of his uncle had hung in the old Burkhead Church and he wondered if I could show him where it was hanging now. He wanted to show it to the lady justice.

"Yes," I said, "let me bring it to you. You stand here inside the door and I will go get it." I left them there with my eight-year-old and went scrounging in that closet to find that portrait. There were old Christmas decorations and out-of-date Sunday school material and Boy Scout tents, and somewhere down there I knew that Brother Burkhead lurked. I finally laid hands on him, and swung around, blowing the dust off of him and came face to face with the chief justice. He had not stayed where I put him in the company of my son. "Well, here it is," I said disingenuously, "apparently, we haven't put it up yet." Which, while being a true statement, did not mitigate my embarrassment.

Several years later, I was assigned to a parish in Charlotte, North Carolina. After the announcement in the newspaper of my impending move, I received a gracious letter from the chief justice, welcoming me to Charlotte and apprising me of the fact that I was to become his pastor, and perhaps I would remember him as the man who came looking for his uncle's portrait, which I subsequently "dug out of a closet" and from which I "had blown the dust." I remembered.

That is a very real risk, I think, of having your portrait hung somewhere. You wonder how long it will be before you end up in the closet. I have just published this one book as of yet, but already I have this dread of what it must be like to see my book on the sale table.

Life is short. Fame is fleeting. History has a way of re-arranging itself according to the biases of the historian. My picture is hanging in several churches where I have served as pastor. When I go to one of them, it seems odd. I look strangely young. There I am part of a line, not at all the most important thing that ever happened to that church. And the issues of those days that were burning and were important are now largely lost and summed up simply by reporting my name and the years I served. It's like reading epitaphs in a cemetery.

13. A Lot Is at Stake

THIS MORNING, I WENT TO THE CHURCH EARLY AS IS MY custom. It is Sunday. I let myself in the church and walked up a single flight of stairs to my office. I automatically tried to insert my key in the lock, but just the pressure of my hand against the knob pushed the door open.

And I saw my office turned upside down. Every drawer had been rifled, every cabinet opened and emptied. Books were taken from their shelves and scattered. The police surmised that someone was looking for money. There is an idea abroad that the preacher keeps the money taken in offerings in his office. So the designated burgling spot in a church is the pastor's office.

What the thief found in my office was not money, just a lot of old sermon manuscripts and minutes of meetings. Which no one wants. They even bore me. What the thief took was a radio that cost about thirty dollars. The church would never put me in charge of money. Not even my wife lets me be in charge of money.

I tried to gather my stuff and make some sense of it. I realized what a pain it is to keep up with stuff. You have to order it, file it, and dust it. And if it's something more than paper or books, you have to have descriptions or photographs of it for your insurance company or the I.R.S. In preparation for a day like this when someone breaks in and steals it. Or just throws it around. And the breaking, entering, and throwing it around exposes it as the junk it is.

Jesus knew how we all get tied up with and in our stuff. The ancient Jews (and Jesus was a Jew) had devised a way for faithful people to acknowledge their dependence on God; they were to give a tenth of what they earned for the benefit of others.

Building on that premise, Jesus wanted us to understand what our affection for and actual bondage to our stuff might do to us. In Middle Eastern fashion, he sometimes talked in hyperbole. Once he said: "It is easier for a camel to go through the eye of a needle than for someone who is rich to enter the kingdom of God" (Matthew 19:24). Some preachers keep trying to dress that up and talk about how "the eye of a needle" was actually a gate in the wall around Jerusalem, and that while it was difficult for a camel to get through there, it probably wasn't impossible.

I don't believe that; I think Jesus knew how it really is. How much we love our stuff. How it will break up marriages and make families stop speaking to one another. And how some people are sick with desire over it. And how people will drive a hundred miles to buy a ticket in the lottery. And how perfectly nice young men and women will manipulate the stock market or arrange loans for their friends out of corporate funds or embezzle money from their employers.

The image of a camel trying to get through the eye of a needle is a preposterous image, but I think it's a good reading of the situation in which we find ourselves relative to our stuff.

Jesus gave us a way out. He called on us to give away some of our stuff. However, in the case of one man, Jesus is on record as having told him that he would probably have to sell everything he had if he meant to be saved. He had gone too far. He was too deeply in to merely fool around with percentages; he would have to get rid of it all.

This is serious business; a whole lot is at stake.

14. A Precious Thing

S A LAST-DAY TREAT FOR HELPING AT HIS MISSION OUTPOST in the Caribbean country of Haiti, he and his wife took Ruth and me, and the high school and college students of our work team, in a truck—first to the Iron Market (a seething, babbling mass of hands and shouts and goods) and then to a quiet beach circled by coconut palms. Offshore were luxury cruise ships, sparkling in stark contrast to the dark poverty on shore. We were joined later by a group of laughing naked boys who jumped and swam with us in the surf.

In between, there were snatches of conversation. Of how he had studied to be a social worker and did that for a while back home in the States; and how, subsequently, he and his wife had offered themselves to work in an independent Baptist mission there in Haiti while they pondered what the Lord wanted them to do next. He had become the administrator of the hospital where we had been working, cleaning and painting the entire inside of the building. He was also the director of the choir at the mission church. She oversaw the work of women who sewed in one of the self-help industries begun by the mission.

He was tired and discouraged. There were no toilets in the hospital, and patients often got out of bed and urinated in the corners of the rooms. The hospital had built outdoor toilets for the patients and their families, but they wouldn't use them. As fast as we cleaned and painted the rooms, they were immediately soiled again.

Haiti is the poorest nation in the Western Hemisphere. Children beg everywhere. The first night we were there, we gathered in a lobby of our hotel. Two sides of the lobby were constructed of open-work tiles. As we talked, I began to see little black hands extended through the tiles, at various heights. There was no sound, just the ghostly specter of dozens of hands imploring us to give them something.

He talked with me about the poverty of spirit among the people, which was as real as their poverty of goods and money. Eventually he thought that he and his wife would come back to the United States to enter seminary.

Neither of us could quite understand the other's way of speaking of God's will; his was so detailed and specific, mine more general and fluid. But we shared something in common—Jesus. We both knew that Jesus sets people free and we both were trying to make that our business.

So we met at a level deeper than words or theological constructs could convey, down where it really matters. We met as brothers in Christ.

He came the next day with his truck to take us to the plane and our hands touched briefly. Our eyes met intensely. We said "good-bye" but we meant "till we meet again."

It was a precious thing.

15. The Refrigerator

THERE IS SOMETHING UNUSUAL GOING ON DOWN IN ESTILL Springs at the home of Mrs. Gardner. There is an apparition that appears on the door of the refrigerator that she keeps on her porch. Every night about 8:30, when Mrs. Partin turns on her porch light, from a certain vantage point one can see a shadowy figure on the door. Mrs. Gardner lives next door to Mrs. Partin's mobile home. Mrs. Gardner says the figure is Jesus, and that as a matter of fact God told her in a dream that he was going to turn her refrigerator into a television as a sign.

Mrs. Partin is not sure that it is Jesus, and besides that she's getting pretty tired of all the folks who come trooping through her house, because the best place to see the apparition is through her kitchen window, and lots of strangers come through, even using her bathroom and her telephone and leaving drink cans in the sink. Mrs. Partin's son, who is a preacher, is even more skeptical. He has seen the image and thinks it could be Willie Nelson.

Our newspaper has printed several photographs of the phenomenon, because it is believed this may be the first sighting of an image of Jesus on a major appliance.

Several people at our church were discussing this phenomenon before Sunday school yesterday, and different ones of us have seen different things on the refrigerator door. I think it looks like Edgar Allen Poe or Hedy Lamarr with a mustache. Cynthia thinks it looks like the Ayatollah Khomeini, an Iranian despot.

One of Mrs. Gardner's neighbors wonders why, if it's Jesus, it isn't there during the day. Mrs. Partin would prefer that, I think, because all of this notoriety is messing up her sleep. On at least one occasion she and her husband had to leave home in order to get some rest (David Jarrard, " 'Face' on freezer being called a miracle," *Tennessean* [May 29, 1987]: 1A, "From miles they come for miracles," [May 30, 1987]).

I want to be the last one to proscribe where God can or will make Godself manifest. It was on the road to Emmaus that the risen Christ was experienced by some of Jesus' friends and he was recognized later, standing around the fire while they were throwing supper together.

And doubtless, Jesus is in Estill Springs too. I just doubt that I would find him on Mrs. Gardner's refrigerator door. Maybe Jesus is to be found someplace where a mother cares

for her bedridden, disabled child, who was born that way—
a child who can neither stand nor speak and has no control
of her bodily functions. And there is this mother who does
all of that for the child without anger or self-pity. Or perhaps
Jesus is to be found in the company of someone who has
been truly wronged but is able to forgive. Or with someone
who failed to do the truth or made a horrendous mistake, but
decided to start again and has, with amazing courage. In
those places and in many others where love is being lived
and grace abounds, Jesus is present all day in Estill Springs
and not just about 8:30 each evening on Mrs. Gardner's
refrigerator door.

16. The Mopping-Up Brigade

T HERE ARE NOTIONS OUT THERE AMONG MANY OF US THAT ladies of the Victorian era mostly tatted lace, attended to their diaries, and, on occasion, had the vapors.

I have just rediscovered a book given me by my Aunt Bettie, shortly before her death at ninety-one. It belonged to her mother, my paternal grandmother, who died when my father was only three and Aunt Bettie was not yet one. It is entitled *Talks on Women's Topics* and was written by someone named Jennie June (a nom de plume).

Ms. June addressed a number of topics relevant to the life of a late nineteenth-century lady and variously entitled them: "Parlor Courtship," "How to Lean on a Gentleman's Arm," "Why Young Ladies Don't Cook," "How to Get Married," "Have Old Maids a Mission?" and so on.

For all their careful grammar and chaste chatter, they are explicit essays on how to manipulate one's delicate way through a male-dominated world.

One piece entitled "Keeping House" outlines a "system of matrimonial management as complete, and yet so simple that every woman can avail herself of it." Please note the portentous term *matrimonial management*; it has an apocalyptic flair to it.

Ms. June goes on to designate men as "creatures of their stomachs" and declares that "a bit of good or ill humor, which a young wife tries in vain to account for, is generally referable simply to a well or badly digested meal." She adds, "Feed a husband to his liking and you can wear a new bonnet every time the sun shines." What a misanthropic cynic she is!

She concludes by counseling that this knowledge is "part of the wife's legitimate weapon and ammunition of war . . . and woe to her who resigns them to an enemy, which every other woman naturally is, who does not own a similar piece of property."

Diarying and tatting, indeed! Note that the husband is designated "a piece of property."

Gloria Steinem, Betty Friedan, and Kate Millett got a late start. Jennie June was strategizing as early as 1864 using terms like "plan of attack" to outline the procedure and "Governor-General" to identify the lead character. Once she advised temperance of response by declaring that "a sensible woman will graduate her plan of attack according to the object to be obtained; she will not use a heavy cannon or a whole piece of artillery for what could be carried off with a single musket shot." Surely, she is speaking metaphorically.

That lady not only knew her battlefield strategy; she was into Transactional Analysis. We who try very hard now to be sensitive to gender issues sometimes assume that we are on the vanguard of the battle line just because we have learned to use a nonsexist vocabulary, only to discover that we are really just in the mopping-up brigade.

People like Ms. June were out there a long time ago, sensitizing us to the quality of persons and the need to learn how things really work:

> What has been is what will be,
>   and what has been done is
>   what will be done;
>   there is nothing new under the sun.
>   (Ecclesiastes 1:9)

17. A Rich Life

HAVE A WEDDING ANNIVERSARY COMING UP AND I HOPE I don't forget it. Actually, it is *our* wedding anniversary, my wife's and mine, and it is a lot of years. And the reason I have trouble with the date is that it is either the 28th or 29th of June, and our son was born on the 28th or 29th of May, and that confuses the whole thing. Of course, it wasn't the same year. All things considered, we are old-fashioned folk and we followed the protocols.

Anyway, we have this anniversary coming up and the woman I married is still interesting and surprising. She has taken up gardening.

This is the woman who, when we moved to the country in our first parish, bolted upright in the bed the first night that we were there and cried out in the dark, "What am I going to do with my garbage?"

That was the same parsonage that had the clothesline all the way down at the back end of the lot. Done that way on purpose so there wouldn't be any room left for a garden. The logic was, "Why do we need a garden when all those farmers have gardens?" And it worked.

Now she has taken up gardening. She has squash, cucumbers, and tomatoes, and a half dozen herbs in what used to be a flower garden. To be more specific, the vegetables and herbs are squinched in, around, and among the flowers.

For thirty years she taught public school, Sunday school, and sang in the choir. A time or two she played the piano at the revival meeting. Once she and a friend played the piano and organ at the revival meeting. The friend said that on one verse she would play the melody line and he would doodle, and on the next verse he would play the melody and she would doodle. Having spent an appreciable amount of time at revival meetings, I understood what he meant.

She led a book club, taught in the Vacation Bible School, was mother to our children, and once was president of the women's organization in our congregation. At one parish, there were three Sunday school classes that met in our house, including one in the kitchen. She ran around the house on Sunday mornings, cleaning up and setting the venetian blinds so that you couldn't see very well. Now she reads radical feminist publications and is a dirt farmer. But she still worries about how ugly her gardening shoes are.

Staying alive is a lifelong project and is more than simply

breathing. It is keeping an interest in this remarkable world of ours with its variety of people and things to do. People who stand around with nothing coming up are as close to dying as you can get, drowning in their own boredom.

I have trouble remembering exactly which day is the anniversary of our marriage, but I never forget how interesting that woman has made my life, because her own life is that way. She has taken seriously Paul's letter to the Corinthians, "For all things are yours, . . . the world or life or death or the present or the future—all belong to you" (1 Corinthians 3:21-22). And because her life is rich, so are the lives of those who love her.

18. Fashion

IT's TIME TO BUY MY SUMMER CLOTHES. YOU SEE, I DON'T
buy my clothing in advance of the season. I buy it at the
end of the season. I can't stand to buy an article of clothing until it is marked down twice.

It's time now. I need some new sports clothes. It's not that
I am deeply into sports, but a shiny black suit and a frayed
white shirt don't do it at a lot of late summer soirees.

I went shopping last night and made some discoveries. All
new swimsuits are yellow, red, blue, and purple (all at once)
and come to the knees. They look funny with black knee sox
and brogans. And many of the casual T-shirts have numbers
on them and stop just below the chest. Which probably looks
terrific on some mid-adolescent whose stomach is firmly
fashioned and in its right place, but you should see one on a
man with a belly lopped over a pair of those long swimming
trunks and over-the-calf black socks.

There seems to be no justice in the way things work. Back
when I had one of those svelte bodies, we wore baggy pants

and shirts that looked like parachutes. Now that bodies are displayed, mine has let loose and gone lumpy.

Fashion is a curious category. We spend lots of money and even more time getting ourselves into it. Which means getting ourselves to look like everyone else at any given time. We dare not be different, dare not look out-of-date or out-of-place. Following fashion fanatically is a dead give-away that we aren't very comfortable with ourselves. And so we put on disguises. And then no one can tell. No one knows how insecure or unhappy we are. By some sartorial sleight-of-hand, we blend safely into the passing social scene like a chameleon. Or so we think.

19. The Rules

RUTH AND I HAVE JUST RETURNED FROM A CONTINUING education event held in Aspen, Colorado. You have to hunt hard for a continuing education event in July in Aspen, Colorado. When the airfares are down.

It was a good experience. The seminar itself, "Themes of Spirituality, Old and New" was challenging and informative. And being 8,500 feet up in the Rocky Mountains in a tony little place like Aspen wasn't bad either. And on our way out, we stopped in Vail for a couple of nights. You see, in order to get the cheap fare, you have to stay over a Saturday night; you do understand that, don't you?

Anyway, in this little hotel in Vail, there were signs all over the place: "No smoking!"; "No one under the age of 25 may register in this hotel!"; "Do not steal the towels and washcloths!"; "No smoking in the halls!"; "Do not slam the doors!"; "Do not put your skis in your room!"; "No smoking in the stairwells!"; "If you plan to be out after 11:00 P.M., take your key!"; and my favorite, etched in brass in the breakfast room, "Take all you want but eat what you take!"

I felt right at home. I thought my mother must have passed through there sometime. It was reminiscent of the "oughts" I grew up with. And I must say that it was a very quiet and orderly little hotel; Mama knew what she was doing.

The hotel in Aspen, by contrast, was a jaunty little European sort of place with no rules. The hot tub was just outside our window, and the first night there were children in it until twenty minutes before midnight, and the next night a different set of children until 11:30 P.M. Where was Mama when I needed her? The management and I finally worked out a deal and all went well thereafter.

It is all a parable of the struggle between fixity and freedom, restraint and license. It is a tale related to Nietzsche's theory of the "will to be responsible to ourselves." It is a basic human struggle—learning to be answerable without coercion. And it is a spiritual struggle that we all experience.

And it is interesting, I think, that we never get it completely right; that we never achieve that state of rulelessness that we would all aspire to. There is still a wildness in us, a will to power, a resistance to domestication that the early theologians labeled "original sin." We contend with it to the end, I think.

It is God alone who finally relieves us of the burden, not by taking responsibility from us, but by allowing us to shoulder it and move on, forgiven.

On my last day in Vail, I noticed that one of the rubber runners on the steps in the stairwell was coming loose in such a way that it was possible it could trip someone. I thought that I would post a sign that proclaimed: "Repair this step immediately or I will smoke a cigarette in your stairwell!" Only I didn't have a cigarette. And, of course, I don't smoke.

I did leave part of a Danish at breakfast.

20. My New Doctor

I LIKE MY NEW DOCTOR. I CAN INTIMIDATE HIM. BY LOWERING my voice and speaking distinctly and looking him squarely in the eye, I can make him pay attention. Always before in these relationships, I was the intimidatee. Physicians have this way of cocking an eyebrow and looking smug while they are adjusting the weight on the scale—up. Or just by being so maddeningly patient when you admit that the reason your cholesterol is up is because you had two eggs over easy for breakfast this morning. With sausage.

The first time I visited my new doctor I was a little surprised at his youth, and while he was out of the room I checked his credentials and discovered that he was the same age as one of my children, who had just recently learned to throw dirty clothes in the hamper and not to put wet towels on the furniture.

There are qualities about him that are a little unnerving. He remembers everything you ever tell him and he sometimes uses that against you.

I have always been a little casual about my doctors. You don't want them to think that they have any power over you. And so you adopt a somewhat jaunty attitude as you tell them what you have and how to treat it. I do recall, however, how a previous physician cut me off at the knees. He was going over the details of a recent physical examination and discussing the issues that needed addressing, when he asked, "Are you going to lose weight?"

Now before I go any further with this story, you need to know that this man was approximately the same age as I, a member of my congregation, and also very possibly my best friend. Anyway he said, "Are you going to lose some weight?" and I flippantly responded, "Probably not." And as he left the examining room, he said, "Get yourself another doctor."

I sat there for a while relishing the exchange, but sitting there in the altogether I began to get chilly. He didn't come back, and so I cracked the door just little bit and as his nurse passed I asked, "Ora Lee, where's Bill?" She responded, "Oh, he's with another patient."

I decided to give him another chance and I did reduce my weight.

None of my doctors has ever accepted my diagnoses. I told this new one that I have arthritis and he didn't give me one bit of argument. He did call in his nurse to give me a shot which made my arthritis (which he called tendonitis) quit hurting. He must not have understood what I said.

The supreme value is to be in charge of all human interaction. But staying in charge isn't easy. Because there are people like traffic cops and I.R.S. agents and headwaiters and psychotherapists to keep you humble. And doctors who know all about you and what you are really like, who keep trying to make you feel better anyhow. In psychological circles, it's called acceptance. In church, it's called grace. And sometimes it's harder to receive than any gift—the unmerited acceptance of another person who has your well-being at heart.

21. A Late Autumn Afternoon

WHAT IS IT ABOUT AMERICAN FOOTBALL THAT OUR population finds so fascinating? It is a wildly brutal sport.

The season, which isn't as easy to define as it once was, is upon us. Thousands of us go to various stadiums and sometimes to plain old fields to watch muscular young men push their way up and down the field and slug it out over possession of a very oddly shaped ball.

My friend from Norway said when we first took him to an American football game: "We have these in Norway; we call them gang fights!" He was accustomed to what Europeans call football, only we know it as soccer. Actually, soccer is a very physical game too but with certain refinements. The players are not required to savage one another. That is done by spectators who fight with other spectators.

My limited experience as a player of football has been in occasional pickup games here and there, and once or twice on my college fraternity's intramural team, where I was in charge of good times.

In one parish, it was the custom of some neighborhood high school boys to gather on Sunday afternoons on the expansive lawn of our church, where they played "tag" football without equipment and the strict rule that no tackling was to take place. Ha!

I went down there once in the late afternoon and, try as I did to stay out of it, I found myself caught up in the excitement, and before I knew it I was in the fray. There was this one kid, seventeen years old and solid as a rock, who seemed always lined up opposite me. At first I wasn't sure but I thought he was getting some kind of kick out of hitting me. Hard.

I couldn't imagine why he would want to do that, but just in case, I would assign myself to another position. Someplace where he wasn't. I would look up and discover that he had reassigned himself opposite me. Where he could hit me hard. It was unspoken but it was real. It may have been against the rules to tackle, but he was getting the most out of his blocks.

That late autumn evening, my football career came to a conclusion when he broadsided me so hard that when I looked up, I couldn't tell which team was mine. Or where the church was. I remembered that I had some mature thing to do in the church and took myself out of the game.

I suppose that is what football is about, in its essence. It is an acceptable way of venting aggression. It beats gang fights and war. That boy and I had an amiable personal relationship but he needed somehow to take on the authority figure in me. We were friends who could talk about significant things. The friend wasn't the person he was knocking around. It was the preacher who knew so much. Or at least, acted as if he did. Getting up in the pulpit, dressed up funny, and telling everybody how it is. Nobody is that smart, or that good. Get him!

I understood. I understand. It has made a more sensitive preacher of me. I really don't know more than the others. I am the one who has been given time to think about life, and a mandate to share my thoughts with the rest. But the flow is both ways. I am instructed and inspired by those very ones whose care has been entrusted to me.

I have discovered that my young friend's tribe is legion. There are others who hang around churches who are willing to engage me at the drop of an ought. He taught me that their hostility isn't personal.

The last I heard of my young adversary, he was doing a residency in surgery in a well-known medical center. He had learned to discipline and direct his energies into healing ministries.

I wonder if he ever goes out among the wild things in his neighborhood on a Sunday afternoon to share his waning energies. If so, there is probably some husky kid out there who isn't all that impressed with his "M.Deity" and who gets a kick out of knocking his socks off.

22. The Vigil

T ODAY, AT A FLOATING PARTY, I RAN INTO A FRIEND WHO attends another church in our city. By "floating party" I mean the kind of party where the guests float from room to room and conversation to conversation.

She asked me if at my church we were "deep into Lent," which is the kind of question you ask the preacher when you run into him at a floating party. I've arranged for baptisms; stood between two women who were trying to schedule their respective daughter's weddings for the same day; outlined the previous Sunday's sermon; fixed it so that a Philippine diplomat's son could go to work as an apprentice cook at the Tulpenfeld Hotel in Bonn, Germany; and made six pastoral calls—all at floating parties.

I responded to my questioner by saying that I thought we were pretty deep into Lent, and then she proceeded to get into her real conversation topic, which was how deep into Lent they were at her church. Which she didn't like. She said that they had no processional during Lent; they had no flowers during

Lent; they don't sing the "Gloria" during Lent; they don't schedule weddings during Lent; and that last Sunday the choir sang a song about smashing babies against the wall, which no doubt was based on something in the Old Testament.

I told her that while we were deep into Lent, we weren't all that deep.

Next week is the week we call Holy, though an awful lot of unholy things took place during it. It is imperative, I think, that we keep Holy Week, if we fully intend to appropriate Easter. We cannot glory in Christ's triumph over death if we have not experienced the reality of his death. His real death. His shameful, painful, messy death. Which he went through alone. None of his male friends was there at the end. Some went to sleep and some ran away. Peter lied about knowing him. He was left alone.

There was no sense of triumph in his dying. Everything had come unraveled and all his hopes were dashed—like babies against the wall. Doubtless, he felt a little silly and in a lot of pain. He cried. First he prayed that he wouldn't have to do it, and then he poured out his feeling of abandonment and queried, "Why?"

And he died.

They are probably on to something at that other church. They are going to be glad to see Easter come. They will probably hurry there on Easter morning.

23. The City

TODAY THE AIR CONDITIONING IS OFF HERE AT THE CHURCH. We have been doing without it for the better part of two weeks because we are installing a new cooling tower, and so I have opened my window.

I had forgotten how the world sounds, having been shut up all these years. It is very noisy out there. There is the rumble of trucks and other heavy equipment, shifting gears as they struggle up the hill. There are children at play on the church playground; and also, there is an agitated motorist who is blowing his horn. There are airplanes, other people's air conditioners, and an exceedingly loud roar that might be the world's biggest vacuum cleaner sucking out the sewers.

And all that is heard by a guy who is hearing-impaired. It must be a cacophony to those who aren't.

An ambulance is passing with a pulsing alarm that momentarily kicks up my anxiety.

These are not just noises, of course; they are the sounds of life. Happy sounds and scary sounds, the whoop that accompanies the drama of everything that is happening out there. Where lives intersect and commerce is in gear and children are rehearsing their lives and emergency rooms are receiving people who are dying right now.

I can't hear them but I know that in the offices that encircle our building, and in the classrooms and labs of the university across the street, there are struggles for power and place that sometimes work themselves out in one-upmanship and treachery. And there are students who, at the same time they are deciding who they are, must make decisions about a life vocation and how they will responsibly handle their sexuality. If the internal stress that is experienced in those places could be heard, it would probably surpass all the other din.

There goes a motorcycle. A big motorcycle. And here comes another ambulance.

We construct our lives in such a way as to block out the shriek and moan of that world. We couldn't bear the pain of it, I think, if we had to confront it all, unfiltered and undifferentiated. So we withdraw behind closed and draped windows or move to the suburbs.

But the drama plays on and it will be enacted here in the inner city, even if we aren't here. Others are and it is they who in the heat will with bitter passion act out their distress. And then we shall have to pay attention.

We must pay attention to the city, not just our city, but all the cities that have not yet learned to cope with the circumstances that have issued from the decline of heavy industry and farming and the migration and joblessness that have ensued.

The noise level is rising and we must pay attention.

A Domino's Pizza delivery person, exiting the parking lot, has just brushed the bumper of a $50,000 car traveling north on Louise Avenue. The driver of the big car, who is wearing a dark suit and black shoes, is vexed but is behaving with considerable self-possession. You can tell how perturbed he is by observing how frantic his motion is as he rubs the spot of impact with a white handkerchief. He and the driver of the delivery vehicle don't seem to be making much headway in their discussion and I'm afraid that pizza isn't going to get delivered in thirty minutes. That's two dollars off, you know. Neither of those men is having a good day.

I am reminded of something that Charlie Brown once said, "That would be nice." He had just heard someone say that, in life, you win some and you lose some.

24. Roger

RECEIVED A NOTE FROM ONE OF MY COLLEAGUES ASKING ME IF I could see a young man who had a request of me. He had been attending our worship with some regularity, though I had never met him and didn't even remember seeing him. He wanted a conversation with me. I said OK and my assistant set up the meeting.

He arrived at the appointed time, a tall slender and blond young man in his mid-twenties. Initially reticent, he got down to the business at hand. He identified himself as gay, and then paused. After a moment, I said, "Yes?" and then he continued. He had moved to our city from another state about a year previous and his parents were coming to visit for the first time. It was time, he thought, to tell his parents about his sexuality and could he bring them there, to my office, and in my presence make this disclosure? They were of our denomination; his mother was active in her church and he had told them that he sometimes attended worship with us.

I told him that I would meet with them and we set a day and hour. Another pause; there was another piece of the story that he thought we ought to discuss. "I have a lover," he said, "and I want to tell my parents that we live together. He won't be there; he is going to stay with friends while they are visiting me."

I said, "OK, we will tell them that also."

Another pause, more pronounced, and I waited. "He's black. My friend is black. My parents are very old-fashioned." Longer pause. I asked, "Do you mean that they will not approve of your relationship with a black man?"

"Yeah, that will be hard for them."

"All right, we have our agenda," I responded, encouraging him to be positive, and comforting him with my hunch that they would not be terribly surprised and would probably be glad to get the topic on the table.

After a prayer together, we stood and he prepared to go. He hesitated again and said, "There is one more thing." Another pause, and then, "I'm a transvestite. I earn a lot of prize money, dressed in women's clothes, in beauty contests in drag clubs all over the eastern United States."

"I'll tell you what," I said without a pause. "Let's just hold that piece of the story for another time." I realized that I had wandered into unfamiliar country and my life maps hadn't been developed to the point that this encounter would require.

The day came. He and his parents came together into my

office. After introductions, I took the initiative and said: "Roger has called this meeting; he has something to tell you," and Roger told them.

It was hard; they had not previously thought that he might be gay. At least, that is what they said. His father thought that if Roger would just find a girlfriend, things would sort themselves out. His mother's voice began to rise. She couldn't work this information into her theology, which was firmly fixed. She obviously felt personally assaulted by his story; she was angry. She didn't know why he would choose such a "lifestyle"; it wasn't the way he was raised and it wasn't the way people in their part of the country lived.

I offered some statistics about the rate of incidence of homosexuality in the population and assured them that Roger declared that it was not a choice; he had known he was attracted to men since childhood.

Roger began to cry and asked them, "Why would I choose this?"

His mother became shrill. His father seemed to be more amenable, better able to process what he was hearing. He said clearly that he didn't understand but that Roger was his child and he would always love him. He said it as if he had thought of it before, as if he had at some previous time made a decision.

When Roger's mother heard what the father said—when what he said sank in, she was aghast, and she said to me with a cry, "That's easy for him to say! He's not a Christian!"

25. Breakthroughs

AREN'T YOU GLAD THAT NOW THAT YOU ARE GROWN YOU don't have to do some things just because you are supposed to? Like eating black-eyed peas on New Year's Day or waiting until Christmas to open your gifts? Or eating a well-balanced meal before you can have dessert?

I was raised in a curriculum of "supposed-to's." I was fourteen years old before I tasted my first Coca-Cola and I had to finish off a glass of milk before I was allowed a glass of iced tea. My brothers and I wore long underwear when nobody else did, and speaking of "oughts," you ought to try to sneak that stuff off and on in a school locker room, hoping no one else will see. I wouldn't go swimming at the YMCA in Cincinnati when my friend took me there, because I didn't want anybody to know I had it on.

Once, our fourth grade basketball team was playing and I didn't have time to get the underwear off, so I pushed it way up high under the basketball shorts. Only, one leg got away and came tumbling down while I was running down the court. I would have welcomed death.

The next game, I just took the stuff off and threw it in a corner. We won the game and I was so excited that I forgot to retrieve it and went home without it. Mama noticed and I had to walk back to school for it. I just threw it over my shoulder and sauntered home. I realize now that was a breakthrough day.

Later on, I discovered that being responsible is important but it isn't the whole story. Life is meant to be enjoyed too. It isn't simply a list of "shoulds" and "should-nots." Being really grown up is knowing the difference between responsible living and rules-keeping.

Jesus was wearied by the rule-keepers and when he rubbed out a handful of grain to eat on the Sabbath, he let his critics know that the Sabbath was made for people and not the other way around. Once, at a wedding, he whipped up some wine when they ran out. Another time, he turned the crowd's wrath away from a woman taken in adultery. He was no dour demagogue just waiting for people to trip over an obligation.

Now that I'm grown up, I can eat my dessert first if I want to. And pass up the black-eyed peas. At our house, we open our gifts as they arrive; I learned that from Ruth. And I have discovered that in bone-chilling weather, there is nothing like long underwear to keep you warm.

26. Maybe Next Time

THINK THAT IF I HAD IT TO DO OVER AGAIN, I WOULD DO IT differently. Live the Christian life, that is. It would be a lot easier and more fun. I wouldn't be nearly as concerned with orthodoxy nor as judgmental as I was the first time. I think I would keep my eyes focused more on expressions of love than ordering by rules. I am aware of the dangers of reducing the great faith to premises that are merely relative—what is measured in terms of how much love my little life can muster. That can't be the love by which I measure my behavior or the actions of others.

I mean instead the self-emptying, disinterested love of God as it was expressed in the life of Jesus, who all the time had time to talk with Mary, Martha's sister; to talk with the woman at the well; to have lunch with the community crook; to stop and deal with a woman by the road who grabbed at the hem of his robe; to go to a wedding where he helped with the refreshments; and to work out some plans with his disciples for a major lunch when a crowd of five thousand showed up to listen to him. Humane things, everyday things. Touching, healing, redemptive things.

Don't misunderstand. I think serious theologizing must go on. I think it is very good that some people have devoted their lives to systematically thinking through a belief system. But I have discovered that merely understanding that system does not necessarily mean that one can appropriate it. Make it work.

The next time, I would want to be more aware of the pleasure of living out the faith rather than forever dodging its hazards and obstacles. I would like to play to my strengths, and circumvent cynicism. I want to accept people as they are, forget how I'm going to look, and be willing to be taken. Even by an accomplished con-man with a classy little scam.

Let me tell you a story.

Early Sunday morning, a Vanderbilt University Hospital medical resident called. His father had died Saturday night and he needed forty-eight dollars to finish paying for his plane ticket home. There were a few oddities in his story, not the least of which was why a Vanderbilt Hospital resident *in extremis* had no financial resource other than a neighboring church. Not his.

When he came to pick up the money, he was dressed in green operating-room scrubs, carrying medical books and wearing a stethoscope around his neck, which he offered to leave as collateral. We waived the collateral; he took the money.

The next morning, on a hunch, I called the medical school; no one by that name is enrolled. I called the hospital; there is no resident by that name. I laughed.

I had been bested in the great guessing game of determining who are the deserving poor, but it didn't bother me. I realized that I actually admired his chutzpah. What a story! It was intricately fashioned and he was in costume.

Meanwhile, I admit, he did a number on us and it was funny. True, he exploited our need to be helpful but no doubt he did need the money. I don't know which parts of his story were true. Maybe he did need to get home. Maybe he wished he were a medical resident but couldn't be—wouldn't discipline himself. Maybe his needs were not what he said they were, but he had needs nonetheless.

The nice part of the story, for me, was not having to feel foolish about it.

I do wish we had taken him up on leaving his stethoscope as collateral. There is probably some medical services employee in our six-hospital neighborhood who is looking for that.

27. Sleepless Nights

I'VE BEEN HAVING TROUBLE GETTING TO SLEEP LATELY. IT never used to be that way. I could astound everyone with my maddening ability to go to sleep. When everyone else was anxious and uptight, I would lie down and sleep.

Not without people making snide comments, of course, remarks intimating that I obviously didn't understand the seriousness of whatever was going on. Or how callous I was, or how sleep is sometimes an escape mechanism, a way of denial. "Are you paying attention?" they would demand of me.

But not lately. Of late, I hate to see night coming. I hear the noise of the air conditoner on hot nights. Or I perspire on the hot sheets with the window open, through which I can hear one neighbor's excited dog and another's wind chimes. They are perhaps the loudest wind chimes on the North American continent. And I can hear trains in the distance and trucks on the interstate. There is an occasional siren or an errant burglar alarm, probably set off by some forgetful homeowner, or somebody's ham radio or the dew.

I lie there. I fret about some tasks that are programmed for tomorrow and I drag up my failed relationships and my dropped responsibilities. I fret about war in Iraq and abused children and drug gangs in urban ghettoes. I fret.

In my out-of-bed hours, I sometimes read things written by Michel Quoist, a French priest. Today I ran across the following in a little book called *With Open Heart.* He wrote it for me:

> There is noise in silence. I already knew that, but I experienced it almost physically last night. It was overwhelming.
>
> I went to bed very late. The whole house was asleep; so were the streets and the city. Not a sound. And yet words and ideas that went round and round in my head and my heart like the traffic in rush hour: traffic jams, honking, shouts, exasperation. I decided to stop this racket. Eyes shut, I concentrated on my breathing. I breathed deeply, slowly. I felt life penetrating me: communion with nature, the vital link with the universe. And one by one the noises disappeared, the silence was silent once again and I felt God move faintly. He was there. I said good morning and good night to him and went to sleep. ([New York: Crossroad, 1983], p. 156)

Of course! That's the way I used to do it. I used to lay me down, and simply turn the whole business over to God. It all belongs to God anyway.

But I forgot. We forget. Now that I am a big deal and have been put in charge of so many things, I am like many of you who really do think that so much of what happens or doesn't is our responsibility.

Tonight I want to remember that business about allowing life to penetrate me, and the part about getting in touch with my vital link to the universe.

Written there on the page, it looks somewhat mystical, but it isn't. It is no more than what I used to do when I simplistically said: "Well, that's it for today, God! Here is the playbook; I'll let you hold it until tomorrow."

I am aware of my big responsibilities in this world. I like having them. What I sometimes forget is that the power of God, God's very presence, is also mine. What keeps me awake can be seen differently when viewed through *our* eyes.

28. Lord of the Dance

A FEW NIGHTS AGO, RUTH AND I WERE DOWNTOWN. AFTER dinner in a restaurant with friends, we came out on the street and heard the sounds of music and laughter coming from the Legislative Plaza. Music on a moonlit summer night has seductive powers. We were drawn to it.

We found the Establishment, a well-known local dance band made up of professional men from our city who also like to make music. They were playing for a dance to which the community had been invited. It was another in a year-long series of events called Tennessee Homecoming, but this one had a special emphasis. A huge banner tied across the columns of the War Memorial Building proclaimed that "Tennessee Homecoming Is for Everybody" and underneath was the name of the sponsoring agency, the Nashville Association for Retarded Citizens.

They were there. A crowd of them. Some so severely brain-damaged that they were strapped into their wheelchairs. Caregivers had brought them from group homes, institutions, and private homes to a dance given in their honor.

The music was great but the dancing was better. Some danced alone, some clung to each other and moved around the plaza, and some of those confined to wheelchairs held hands and swayed their bodies to the beat. They were unaware of or unconcerned about gender, color, or age. One group had circled up and individuals would take turns getting into the center of the circle and improvising wonderfully inventive dance steps.

Everybody smiled. I, who have difficulty remembering which is the right foot and which is the left, was drawn into the joy of the occasion and took my Ruth for a whirl around the plaza. Lost in the celebration of life.

I think that must be what real dancing is. A spontaneous expression of gladness. That's the kind of dancing David did when he danced before the Ark of the Covenant. It wasn't something he learned in fifteen lessons at Arthur Murray's. It was elation and exultation and delight in God that moved his limbs.

I thought about those people of whom the sign said, in effect, life is for everybody. I watched them dance. They didn't do it well; they did it better than I had ever seen it done. They were celebrating themselves. For whom not much in this world works because it is geared to the rest of us who have different levels of understanding and skill than do they. But for one night, at least, there was a dance for them—by them.

I looked carefully to see who was with them, helping them and making sure that no one was left out. Later, the helpers would have to take them home, bathe them, and help them to bed. Those caregivers are servants of the Lord of the Dance.

In our rush to get our budgets balanced and our military hardware in place, it is easy to slough off sound programs that somehow include a summer night's dance on the Legislative Plaza. For folks who never get asked to dance. It's one of the easiest items to cut from our budgets because in the world's economy, it doesn't pay its own way and produces no measurable product. Just happy faces.

What is there to defend or come home to if home is not for everybody?

29. Dubai

HAVE YOU EVER BEEN RUMMAGING THROUGH DRAWERS OR boxes and, while looking for something else, found something you not only had forgotten but had never seen before, and you had no idea whence it came, or why?

I found such a thing last night in a file box on top of my study desk. It's a brochure for the Ramada Inn in Dubai. That's a city in the United Arab Emirates, a remote Arab place in the Persian Gulf. It's not far from Iran and Oman and Yemen. Which is actually pretty far, because in that part of the world, everything is far.

I am reminded of what Mr. Clemmer, an elderly neighbor of ours in my growing-up years, once said about Cincinnati, Ohio, after his first visit there. He opined that he didn't think it would ever amount to much because it was too far away from everything. I think Dubai is like that.

What I am most interested in, however, is where I got that brochure. And why. And though it is partially printed in Arabic (or Farsi, or Syriac, or Urdu, or something) I wonder if the people who run Dubai know that in the brochure one is invited to "have a pre-dinner drink at Dirty Nelly's Pub." And also "for those of you who prefer a little more action [they] have the Black Gold Club." In Dubai, I think that would be like setting up bar at a Southern Baptist Convention.

Anyway, I have never been to that part of the world and never planned to go there, and consequently I wonder how such a brochure came into my possession.

I shouldn't be surprised, because I have a lot of stuff like that, not just in my files but in my head. We like to think of ourselves as lucid folk who behave in rational ways. The truth of the matter is that there are a lot of unexamined presuppositions by which we live. Not many of us live that altogether reasonable life we would like others to see in us.

Little bits of irrationality and prejudice show up in the wisest of us, like a wayward travel brochure among our personal effects. One that seems to indicate our itinerary. But doesn't.

It is no doubt confusing to those with whom we live, when in the midst of some crucial conversation we detour to "Dubai" without even signaling a turn. Because we have our minds cluttered with unexamined trivia and untruths. Every mind needs ordering, our assumptions examined, and our ignorance challenged.

Incidentally, if you are ever in Dubai, the telephone number is 10, which, if you are paying attention, ought to tell you something about the place.

30. A Moment of Song

W HILE I WAS IN AFRICA, I FOUND MYSELF BEING stimulated almost continuously, and by several things at once. So much was going on that it was hard to be aware of everything.

It wasn't part of the agenda, but one night after work, several of us walked out to the camp of some of the workers who were building a new building at our agricultural project in Zambia. They had finished their labors for that day, had gone to the river to bathe, and were preparing their supper over an open fire. They had set up a makeshift camp where they slept on boards or mats and kept around them a few things like a pot and food supplies. Including a Coca-Cola bottle full of long worms!

The unusual thing—the thing that caught my eye and ear—was a musical instrument they had fashioned out of wood and vines and dirt. It was a very primitive instrument and, at the same time, a very sophisticated one.

It was built xylophone-fashion over a hole dug out of the ground. It had sixteen boards, hand hewn, laid across the hole, which was deep and wide at one end. Each board, when struck with a handmade wooden mallet, gave off a clear, resonant tone.

I couldn't figure exactly what the scale was but it was fashioned in such a way that there were never any atonalities, even if you struck two notes side by side.

Three men played it at once, squatting beside it and tapping out marvelously syncopated rhythms with a simple but intoxicating repetition.

At first I was drawn by their music and even tried my hand at it but could never get the proper beat. Then I switched my attention to the men themselves—young with muscular bodies that glow purple-black like eggplant. They have wide eyes in high-cheekbone faces—faces that light up when they smile. They are shy and self-effacing and they work hard. But when night comes and supper is over and they have bathed, they squat there beside that remarkable instrument making music.

And I thought: *Where do they get it? How do they know how heavy to make the mallets and how deep and wide to dig the hole? And how do they do it without directions that say "part A fits into part B, which fits into part C"?*

And where do they get their songs? Songs soft and sweet, civilized and civilizing—no jerky primal rhythms here. Instead they are gentle, soothing, caressing sounds.

96

And I thought: *They get it from the Great Musician who puts the songs in their hearts. They get it from the same Source who sends them each night to bathe in the crocodile-infested Zambezi River with a bar of soap, procured through a thirty-eight-mile walk and a bridgeless river crossing, and a significant sense of self. They get that from the Great Self.*

It was a moment of truth; a moment of song!

31. Important People

SEE THAT PRINCESS ANNE IS COMING TO TOWN. I HAVE always thought that it is the height of notoriety to be known by one name only. Just *Ann*. Or is that *Anne?* If you have only one name, you want it spelled correctly. I think she has a last name. It probably is Windsor, which isn't her name really. Her real name is a German name, because the British royal family is actually German. I'm a little confused about the German name—it could be Saxe-Coburg, which was the name of Queen Victoria's husband. Victoria was one of Ann/e's grannies. The name could be Battenberg, which became Mountbatten about the time of the First World War because the British were at war with the Germans, and you don't want your royal family carrying around an enemy name.

Or was Mountbatten the name of Ann/e's father, not her mother? And while ordinary people generally take their father's name, do British princesses? Probably not.

Anyway, she is coming to town. To ride a horse. And there

seems to be considerable excitement about it. Maybe there will be some parties around for her and I will get to speak to her. I met her mother once at a reception. She probably told Ann/e about me. I was the one who tried to slip out early in order to give my ticket to my wife so she could come in and meet the Queen. We had only one ticket and devised this elaborate scheme where we could both get in on that single ticket. Only we didn't know the rules. Nobody leaves a party before the Queen leaves. That's what the two big guys just outside the door told me when I attempted an exit. And I had no reason to think they were putting me on. They didn't seem very jokey.

Beside that, Ruth had been in church when the Queen came in. Ruth was sitting on the aisle and Elizabeth (that's what we call her) processed right by her. Afterward Ruth said, "I was so close I could have tripped her!" Some of us thought that was a funny thing to say and I was glad that the two big guys outside the door didn't hear her say it.

All of this took place at John Wesley's church in London on the occasion of its reopening in 1978 after a long rehabilitation. It was the first time a British Sovereign had ever entered a Methodist church, because Methodists had always been considered dissenters against the Church of England. By the way, Phillip (that's Ann/e's father) read the Epistle lesson. He did very well and pronounced all the words right.

Once, when I was pastor of the American Church in Bonn, Germany, then-President Jimmy Carter came to worship. A CBS reporter called me on the phone the week previous and asked if any other important people ever came there to church. I told him that they did, every Sunday. When he asked who, I said: John, and Wally and Jiggs, and Rick and Bob and Sharon and Sarah, and . . . he had no sense of humor.

That's the way I feel about Ann/e's visit to our city. I am sure that she is a very nice lady and she wouldn't have been bad looking if they had just had her teeth fixed. But lots of important people regularly come to town, and important people live on my street, and in your house. And some of them even come to church. Regularly.

32. Madan

RUTH AND I FLEW INTO KATMANDU, NEPAL, ON A SUMMER night, just the two of us. We had never been in that part of the world before our plane set down on a runway backed up in the distance by the towering Himalaya mountains. The terminal looked like the bus station in Cheraw, South Carolina, circa 1950.

After we had deplaned and gathered up our stuff, we pushed through the front doors of the terminal, hoping to find someone to drive us to our hotel. What we encountered in the dim glow of a single streetlight was a wall of people, all wanting to carry our luggage, to provide us with transportation, or simply asking for money.

Then out stepped a tall young man who had been told by a mutual friend of his and ours—a German man—that we were arriving on that flight. He approached us and, after calling our names, paused and placed his hands together in a prayerlike position, giving the traditional Hindu greeting "Namaste!" which means "Shalom" as Jews say or "Salaam" as some Muslims say. We twenty-first century Christians have a similar greeting that we exchange somewhat self-consciously to our neighbors prior to receiving the Holy Communion. "Peace," we say.

The young man's name was Madan and he took us to our hotel and told us that he would come for us in the morning to help us accomplish whatever we wanted to do; and then he disappeared into the darkness.

He was in the lobby when we went for breakfast and he engaged a car for us and we began our rounds. It was apparent from the beginning that he was a very religious Hindu and he seemed never to pass an altar or some other holy place without kneeling for prayer, or at least acknowledging the altar with the same hands-clasped gesture as he rode by in the car. At each of the altars there was a small dishlike accessory that held a bright red compound, much the same consistency and color as lipstick.

Usually, after his first prayer in the morning, he would touch his finger to the red compound and then touch it to the middle of his forehead, which of course left a red spot there. It was a sign of devotion to the Great God. Ruth and I would stand aside and wait for him to complete his devotion.

We had a remarkably good time together; he was a very serious young man, at that time studying business at the university. He had come to know our German friend through a German Lutheran organization that puts Western people in touch with destitute children in developing countries. The agency acts as the broker for the giver, whose money then is assigned to a par-

ticular child. Madan's father had died when he was only seven
or eight years of age, his younger brother still an infant.

Once, when our German friend traveled to Nepal, he decided
to find the boy and his family and visit them. He discovered that
the entire family was living on his small monthly contribution.
Because of that, Madan told us, his family survived; otherwise
they would have died. He called our German friend "Father" and
said he was privileged to be of service to "Father's friends."

Our relationship grew, and one morning as he completed
his prayers in front of a roadside altar he marked the red dot
on his own forehead, and then brought the dye and first made
a mark on Ruth's forehead and then on mine, after which he
bowed, folded his hands, and blessed us with "Namaste!"

I cannot tell you how affecting that was. Here was this
splendid young man who, we discovered, had taken an all-
day bus ride to be with us in Katmandu and was missing his
university classes. And now, with a single act, he had drawn
us into his world by including us among the faithful.

Everywhere we went that day, people opened doors for
us; they smiled at us; they greeted us. As we returned to our
hotel that night, the doorman smiled broadly, performed a
little bow and pointed to his forehead. Because we wore on
our foreheads the sign of a faithful devotee of the Great One,
Brahman, we were no longer merely pale-faced strangers
who spoke oddly inflected English; we were living in the
land of Namaste.

33. Manners

I N JAPAN, WHILE RIDING THEIR BULLET TRAINS, I WATCHED AS the young women vendors on the train would stop at the door of each car as they were exiting. They would turn toward the passengers, make a deep bow, and say something that I didn't understand but which I took to be some parting pleasantry, mandated by social convention.

To my Western eyes, it was an odd thing because no one was paying attention, but it was also a charming thing. And not for reasons of eccentricity, but because it was a little sign of civility in the midst of late twentieth-century urban insensibility.

Manners are indigenous things of course, and if you move around much, you have to stay alert to the change from place to place. Where I grew up in Kentucky, a man shook hands upon greeting another man. You shook hands with a woman only if she offered her hand first. Which she wasn't apt to do. In Germany, you shake hands with everyone in the room upon arrival, and again as you leave. In Nepal and India, one does not touch strangers. You greet them by putting your hands together, and nodding toward them.

The line, or *queue* as the British call it, seems to be an invention of theirs and is generally practiced only where they once empired. Many others push and shove and think you rather stupid if you don't. The British, like the Japanese, are imminently well mannered except when they attend a professional soccer match.

Life moves so quickly and convention changes so fast that one isn't sure just what the appropriate thing is to do or say. If the old rules are taught, there seem to be times when they aren't applicable. Most of us live very complex lives that require a lot of time and concentration. The easiest way to get from point A to point B is often a straight line, regardless of who is standing in the way, or how they may feel about our action. We forget or simply fail to acknowledge that they are there and how they feel about our words or actions.

My mother was big on manners and drilled us on things such as "please" and "thank you" and "yes, sir" and "no, ma'am." It was a little confusing later when I discovered that there were people who didn't want to be called "sir" or "ma'am." They thought it was affected and unnecessarily distancing. "Sir" and "ma'am" went out with "Mr." and "Mrs.," which was about the same time that many people decided they wanted to be known by their first names.

The intricacy of knowing and keeping good manners shouldn't keep us from practicing them, however. I once received some good advice on the subject from a fifteen-year-old girl. I was one of the judges of the Miss North Mecklenburg County contest back when such things were fairly endemic. It was a fundraising event sponsored by a service club. Many of the high school girls were entered.

I sat in on an interview with the girls. They were asked what they thought constituted good manners. This particular young lady answered without hesitation: "It is making another person feel comfortable." She got my vote.

It is much more than that, of course, but it is that. It is treating another person as if he or she is valuable, worth noticing. It doesn't mean sacrificing your own values, of course, or compromising your integrity. It is acknowledging another person.

Jesus was walking through the street one day when he noticed a man named Zacchaeus up in a tree. Zacchaeus had climbed there, presumably, to get a better look as Jesus moved through a crowd.

Jesus stopped, pointed at him, and said: "Zacchaeus, come down out of that tree. I'm going to your house for lunch!" I have often thought of that and how Zacchaeus must have felt hearing his name called, and hearing also acceptance, the wonderfully redemptive sound of acceptance.

Good manners are like that. They put our relationships in context.

34. A New Brother

YESTERDAY I BAPTIZED MY GRANDSON, JAMES LEE. IT WAS in his church in North Carolina but the pastor knows about grandfathers, and so he asked me to perform the sacrament. Those were moving moments for me. I did not grow up in the church and thus I was not baptized until I was an adult. And while it was a meaningful experience and something I wanted very much to do, there is still a wistfulness in me that wishes I had been baptized as an infant when I was even too little to turn over by myself or open the refrigerator door.

It was I who took my grandson and who looked his parents, my children, in the eye and asked them about their profession of faith and whether or not they would nurture James in that faith and by their teaching and example guide him to accept this grace for himself.

And then I put the water on his head and baptized him according to that ancient ritual "in the name of the Father, and of the Son, and of the Holy Spirit." Not necessarily a politically correct ascription these days, but words that roll more easily off my tongue because of these long years of saying them.

And I drew him to me, not just as a grandfather cuddling an infant grandson, but now because he was no longer just that, but more, a beloved brother in Christ. This little bit of protoplasm with the funky hair, my brother in Christ. All of us standing there in front of the body of believers—father, adult children, and child—were more than simply father, adult children, and child. There was a whole lot more going on than family sentiment. We belonged to the great family of God, the body of Christ, our faith having been passed on by generations of believers who lived before us. And through the years that faith had also been confirmed by God's Holy Spirit.

It was our ancestors who had heard the story and, having believed, told it to their children and they now to their children. And yesterday, there we were acting it out again, in the presence of God and the community of faith, making our declaration of faith and our promises of loyalty to God and to one another. And it was sealed by the presence of God. It was sacramental in that it was an outward and visible sign of an inward and spiritual grace—God was present. The Holy God was there. I felt the power of it. James is God's child and to be reckoned with differently because of that.

Unfortunately, James looks like me. Not as I looked when I was three months old but as I look now: no neck, three chins, bags under his eyes, and with a big belly. The good news is that he will grow out of it. With that face full of dimples and huge round eyes, I think he is going to have devastating good looks.

The bad news is that I won't get any better.

35. The Invitation

I AM STILL IN A STATE OF DISBELIEF AS TO HOW I SPENT
yesterday. Today is Monday and I am still suffering the
staggers from Sunday. I am the guest speaker at a church
in another state and the way this thing worked yesterday was
like this: there were identical services at 8:20 A.M., at 9:40
A.M., and at 11:00 A.M.

One crowd exited the front of the sanctuary, and the next
crowd entered the rear. It was like a car wash. Or one of those
theaters at Disneyland, where you go in, sit down, and then the
whole theater moves next door for some performance or other.

It's all very vital here, alive and upbeat. Which is probably
a very good thing for these young adults who seem to be pro-
liferating here. The trouble is this preacher is in some measure tired, and sometimes down. Because, you see, I preached
again last night and have two more sermons today, and again
tomorrow. Not to mention that I am to meet with my men's
Bible group on Wednesday back home; and that evening I
continue the saga of the Dead Sea Scrolls with an adult group.

Being a visiting preacher is a curious thing because I have always thought that the word of faith is a word passed like a contagion among friends, not between strangers.

But here I am, trying to sort through my faith and hoping somehow to help these young people make some connection that will enlarge their lives. A few Sundays ago, I said in my sermon that I thought what was needed right now was preaching. Not a seminar nor a convention but preaching, which is not the spot in which I have always found myself— so much preaching is deadening and judgmental. But I think we still need to hear how to live our lives morally and with a long view. We have of late been too much concerned with what works and with December 31's bottom line.

I have throughout my career been amazed that people will present themselves at worship and sit down and allow me to get up before them and tell them things. As a matter of fact, it sometimes gives me a stomachache and a hurting head. "What," my racing heart telegraphs my brain, "do you have to say that is worth all those human hours?" And the brain responds with, "Why do you have to put it that way?" and immediately signals the back of the head to go into one of those vise holds that almost immobilizes me, and alerts the stomach that it is time to gnarl.

What we are about is that we are, all of us, trying to know God. Trying to experience God and to honor God with our lives. But there is a second part to what is happening, and it is that when we reach out, God accepts the life proffered, just the way it is. We don't have to get good and memorize the rules. God says, "I like you just the way you are!"

And then a remarkable thing happens to the people who have been accepted. They start accepting. They begin dismantling a lot of their categories and find out that they are able to reach out to others. They find ways to help one another that were not previously apparent. And the whole thing is like a party.

Jesus compared it to a party. He said the doors are open; the red carpet has been laid; the tables are set; and the Host smiles warmly and comes to greet us, holding out a hand and saying, "Come up here and sit with me!"

How can I risk not telling people that?

36. The Wall

W ATCHING THE BERLIN WALL COME DOWN, OR AT LEAST come open, was an emotional experience for me. Having lived in Germany for a while and having visited the Wall over a number of years, I had a disaffinity for the way it grew and spread like a deadly infection.

First, it was just barbed wire and boarded-up buildings; then it became a bona fide wall with rounded tile on top, so that people who might want to cross it would have no way to get a grip; then it became a wall and a fence, with a wide strip of plowed and raked earth between the two. And watchtowers with armed guards and snarling dogs. And all of it lit brightly with enough candlepower to flood a football stadium.

How like us! We establish borders in our lives—things we absolutely believe and things we absolutely do not believe— and then we start embellishing them and shoring them up. If the principle seems weak and somebody else's idea challenges it, we just build the wall higher rather than consider some new possibility. We stop cold any flow of information that might help us. We also shut ourselves in along with our prejudices and presumptions. What started out as a way of sorting out truth and organizing knowledge becomes The Way. It is not unlike the Wall that, like Topsy, "just growed."

Watching those young Germans, East and West, scramble over the Wall, and watching them take picks and axes to it, was a cathartic experience for me. Walls need to come down. Categories need to be reorganized.

Christ will do that for us. He is quoted in John's Gospel, as having said, "I am the way, and the truth, and the life" (14:6). And He is! Not in any dogmatic way is he the way, in spite of the fact that his followers have tried through the centuries to nail him down to some manageable creeds. You can't do that to the way, the truth, and the life. Creeds are only proximate; they may help you organize your beliefs but only in a partial way. You must never mistake the creed for the Christ.

Christ is the head of the wall demolition squad. If the Son makes you free, you will be free indeed.

37. The Bridal Consultant

I REALIZE THAT A LOT OF FOLK THINK WORKING AROUND A church is all prayer meetings, potlucks, and fundraising. But it's not. Whatever is going on in your world is going on here too. We get to meet the most interesting, boring, imaginative, dull, devout, sacrilegious, predictable, outrageous, levelheaded, intelligent, dopey people in the world. If you wait long enough and keep your door standing ajar, they will sooner or later show up.

This past week, The Bridal Consultant called. She has a client who would like to be married in our cloister garden. When apprised of the fact that either of the principals in the wedding party (or their parents) must first belong to our church, she was undaunted. Then, she said, she would like to arrange her client's membership in our church.

That was a new thing. Hardly a day passes that some prospective bride, in the company of her fiancé but more often accompanied by her mother, doesn't call or come by with the announcement that she is going to have her wedding here. But we have never before had The Bridal Consultant call to arrange for church membership, as another of the services that she offers along with selecting the bridesmaid's gowns, videotaping the ceremony, booking a Caribbean cruise, and renting a limousine.

It is tough, keeping our faith separated from our culture. And the culture, of course, often shapes the faith. Which is too bad because those first-century Christians meant to do it the other way around. Shape the world. Paul, who was no theological wallflower, said it straight up, "Don't be conformed to this world!"

Now we have this dilemma. How do we tell The Bridal Consultant that there are some things she can't arrange? Like the ever-afterness of her bride and groom; how they will relate to one another; what kind of parents they will be; and the bride's church membership, which is an expression of the bride's faith commitment.

How do you go all the way back and talk about the church, not as a building, but as a community of faith? How do you talk about the sanctity of marriage, and how Christ is present there? How we believe that God has created us for one another, to bring completion to one another, and then asked us to bring a promise to that premise? And how do you explain to The Bridal Consultant that marriage is such a serious commitment that our congregation requires that the couple be counseled about these matters, and that the ensuing ceremony is to be viewed as a service of worship?

How do you tell The Bridal Consultant all that without appearing patronizing?

Or without laughing.

38. Wings to Bear Me Up

I WAS SITTING AT THE DESK OF THE CHURCH SECRETARY ON A Sunday morning when she wasn't there. Her office fronted mine. You passed her desk to enter my office. It was Sunday morning and folks were arriving for Sunday school, and the sound of their gathering was building in intensity. You could hear them greeting one another and checking up on one another's health and how the week had gone.

I was sitting at this desk where I never sat; it wasn't mine. I sat there scratching something out on a piece of paper, I don't remember what. Maybe it was a note to stick on somebody's classroom door. Or maybe a family member called with a message for someone who was expected to be at the church that morning.

For whatever reason, I was there in a place where I usually was not, when I overheard the conversation of a group of women. They had gathered outside the secretary's office and they were talking about the pastor. They were talking about me.

And some of what they said was critical of the pastor; everything said by one of them was pointedly critical of the pastor. I knew her well. She was my friend.

It was one of those awful times that happen now and then in your life. When you feel bad but you have to get up and keep moving and doing whatever it is you are supposed to do, only now the veils are stripped away and you know how it really is—how some people view you, how you are perceived. You can't let it stop you in your tracks because you have to do what you have to do.

But things have changed; you have heard. And there is a part of you that silently protests, "That's not who I am, the person she just described." But there is the part of you that sadly acknowledges, "Maybe I do not know myself."

In either case, friendship is compromised and innocence is vanquished. And one gets on with life, directed by a sadder but wiser understanding of that life. Some relationships can be renegotiated; some remain irreconciled.

I didn't always know that and I tried very hard to put them back together. I went to people and tried to explain myself or to apologize for my imperception and unsympathetic behavior only to discover that I couldn't accomplish it.

I had to learn to live with brokenness and to learn to "sin bravely," as Martin Luther put it.

In the book of Deuteronomy, there is a passage that reads:

> As an eagle stirs up its nest,
>   and hovers over its young;
> as it spreads its wings, takes them up,
>   and bears them aloft on its pinions,
> the LORD alone guided him. (32:11-12a)

You probably thought that was something written by Bette Midler. It is the song of Moses, delivered to the entire assembly of Israel—assembled at the end of his life.

Even in the midst of disappointment and anxiety, my Parent God has done the same for me. He keeps finding me in a wilderness, the wilderness of my own shallow life. She hovers over me, spreading her wings to receive me. She has asked me to let go of my false and empty gods.

With her love for nurturing and his eye for protection, God is both Mother and Father to me.

What an interesting metaphor. When I remember this eagle flight of my life, I feel so loved and so in love that I feel gratefully safe. I can soar above both the hateful characterizations that others make of me, and above my own unworthiness. In my most desperate moments, this is what becomes clear to me, this is what I know: Nothing matters because everything does.

39. A Serenely Unclouded Place

I HAD JUST FINISHED MY USUAL SWIM AT THE YMCA POOL. I felt a little disoriented and couldn't boost myself out of the pool in normal fashion. I crawled out and headed toward the shower but first stopped to shave. I looked in the mirror. My face had given way on the right side and I knew that I must get myself to the emergency room. I called Ruth; she picked me up and we headed to the hospital, only blocks away.

We went in. Ruth spoke to one of the women who was doing intake and she motioned toward some chairs where I could wait. Ruth went to park the car and very soon the woman motioned for me. I said to her, "I think I am having a stroke." Without speaking, she stood up and led me to a nearby curtained space where I was met by a squad of young doctors, nurses, and technicians who took my clothes and began pasting terminals to my chest and hooking up IVs. It was as if I had been delivered into the hands of God. I had peace.

Before I was taken away, a muscled, hard-hatted man was brought in on a gurney. Apparently in pain, he called out,

"Oh! Oh! Oh! Oh! Oh!" in a rhythmic staccato pattern, as a frightened child might comfort himself. In my prayer, I assigned him to the same source, to the same inner place, where I found peace.

It's a place that is difficult to describe and report. There are no formulaic ways to get there; there are no patterns to it; it is not something for which one gets ready. One day you find yourself facing life's ultimate experience. You find yourself up against an event that cannot be resisted. It will not be moved. You cannot go around it.

And in that moment, you find there the God of all creation. It isn't a God who says, "I'm going to save you out of this mess" or "I'm going to set aside all the rules by which the universe works and save you." It's a much bigger and more shattering experience than that. That day, I was poised on the edge of God's Mighty Presence in a serenely unclouded place. The view from there was clear.

It has happened before, not often, not even now and then, but whenever I find myself cornered, stymied, shipwrecked in the shallows of life with a rising tide.

My young compatriot of the curtained cubicle began to grow quiet. As I was wheeled out, I turned to look at him. I hoped to give him some sign of acknowledgment but his eyes were closed. I did a thumbs-up anyway, for myself as much as for him.

He lay there calmly, clad only in gleaming white Jockey shorts. They must have come out of the plastic that very morning. His mother would have been proud.

40. Rejoice!

I WAS PULLING OUT OF A CEMETERY THIS MORNING, HAVING just finished officiating at the funeral of a young friend. I was feeling sad and confused and caught in that peculiar place where one finds oneself immediately after the funeral. That particular life was over; the ceremonies had ended; and now everyone has to get on with their lives.

I was trying to negotiate getting into a fast-moving line of Saturday shopping traffic. Christmas was two days away and vehicles were coming relentlessly from my right and I couldn't see but a very short distance to my left. It was a risky bit of business.

I had turned the radio on without even thinking of it. I suppose that I wanted to get my mind focused somewhere else. There was a gorgeous violin concerto pouring from the speakers. I found myself suddenly engaged at many levels. I was trying to get home through some aggressively disagreeable traffic; deal with the untimely accidental death of a thirty-two-year-old father of two;

think about life's meaning; and simultaneously appropriate a Mozart concerto. The day was blue, bright, and
brisk.

As I maneuvered my car into the midst of that frightening
flow, one man pushed down on his horn, and a middle-aged
woman shot me an obscene gesture. She had been forced to
reduce her speed to less than sixty-five miles an hour on a
city street. Doubtless the two of them were on their way to
or from some Happy Holiday shopping.

What I wanted to do was stop the lady and her coconspir-
ator with the hooter and say, "Listen to this music! Look at
this day! Enjoy it! You will not always have the energy nor
the will to race to and fro in pursuit of your life."

There is so much to manage in life the way we live it.
There are so many things to remember, to do and not to do.
Always there are the rules. We have organized ourselves in
order to make life more manageable and then we curse the
organization. We establish goals to give some meaning and
purpose to our lives and sometimes find out, too late, that
they were the wrong goals. Oh, the goal was OK; it just did-
n't fulfill its purpose. We didn't end up happy. Secure and
correct maybe, but without any joy.

Dear Jesus, I prayed as I drew up to a traffic light, *thank
you for Mozart; thank you for all of those people who spent
years practicing in order to play his music for me now. And
thank you for the radio, and thank you for the blueness of*

the sky, and thank you for the affectionate relationship I had with my friend—now dead—and thank you for this automobile, and thanks, too, for the lady with the red face, and the man with the big horn. Until they came along, I was about to forget the other things.

And thanks, too, Jesus, for granting me the possibility of a fulfilled life. One that may not always be happy, but one that need never be less than joyous.

As I wound my way home, I realized that I was about to get in touch with Christmas. Get in touch with the Spirit that speaks to all of us yet, "Don't be afraid! I have some great good news for you! Jesus is coming! The death of your young friend and your aging life are both redeemed. Rejoice!"

About the Author

RUSSELL T. MONTFORT SPENT HIS LATE CHILDHOOD AND adolescence on a farm in rural Oldham County, Kentucky, where he learned that tending animals and crops is a demanding, always thing. He says he had two burning ambitions: (1) to grow up and (2) to leave that place. He had few details in mind, of his journey or his destination, but he felt sure he would go someplace where the lights were bright and there would be music and laughter and Baked Alaska. (He once read about Baked Alaska in *Ladies Home Journal,* his mother's magazine, and wondered how you could bake ice cream.) He liked to draw and thought that perhaps he would become a commercial artist or own his own advertising agency or maybe he would be a movie star. The closest he ever got to show business was when he became a high school cheerleader, unless you count the time he and Marjorie Pollard played "The Beautiful Blue Danube" as a duet on their accordions at the LaGrange, Kentucky, Rotary Club.

When he finished high school at Funk Seminary in LaGrange, he left. Nobody called the school Funk Seminary but that is what is printed on the graduation diploma. It was known as LaGrange High School because when you are leading a cheer in a district basketball tournament in Kentucky, "LaGrange" probably sounds better. He sometimes thought that using Funk Seminary in a cheer would be really funny, but fortunately he kept it to himself, which he says he did a lot of: keeping things to himself, things he found ironic or absurd.

With a degree from Kentucky Wesleyan College (AB, 1950) and two more degrees from Duke University (BD, 1953; Th.M, 1964) and amended vocational goals, he became a pastor of four rural United Methodist churches scattered over three counties in the piedmont of North Carolina. No bright lights, progressive jazz, or Baked Alaska there. He was right back where he started. There was some subdued laughter and a lot of irony.

He has been married to Ruth Nance Montfort for fifty-two years. They are the parents of Leslie Montfort Marsicano and Joel Montfort and grandparents to three boys: Chris, Jamie, and David. After serving churches in North Carolina and Germany, he retired as pastor of West End United Methodist Church in Nashville, Tennessee. Along the way, there were bright lights in exotic places, some great music, and an occasional Baked Alaska.

He is the recipient of two honorary degrees: DD from Davidson College (1961) and DD from Kentucky Wesleyan College (1982).

In his retirement he volunteers as a child custody advocate for the Children's Law Center in Charlotte, North Carolina, and he and Ruth teach developmentally disabled adults in their church.